WHEN
THE FAT LADY
SINGS

OPERA HISTORY AS IT
OUGHT TO BE TAUGHT

DAVID W. BARBER

WHEN THE FAT LADY SINGS

OPERA HISTORY AS IT OUGHT TO BE TAUGHT

DAVID W. BARBER

SOUND AND VISION

Table of Contents

Author's Note
And Acknowledgements

"The opera's not over until the fat lady sings," goes the saying. And when the fat lady sings, there's sure to be a story or two to tell about that extraordinary pastime Samuel Johnson called "an exotick and irrational entertainment," the opera. (Spelling was not so exact a science in Johnson's day as in our own, that being before the days of spell-checkers and other computerized wizardry.)[1]

When The Fat Lady Sings: Opera History As It Ought To Be Taught is my third foray into the dangerous realm of musical humor, following on the heels of *A Musician's Dictionary* and *Bach, Beethoven, And The Boys: Music History As It Ought To Be Taught* (which, if you don't already own, I would greatly appreciate if you ran out and purchased right away).

As I have earlier done with *Bach, Beethoven,* I feel it important to stress that the historical information you're about to read – I hope you're about to read – is true (or at least has been perpetuated by some other historians before me). As the great Anna Russell is fond of saying, "I'm not making this up, you know!"

Those who've already read *Bach, Beethoven* (thank you) will notice the occasional similarity between that book and this one, for which I make no apologies. It is, after all, the same history. Besides, the history of opera, as you will

---

[1] Johnson was perhaps not the best judge of such matters. His biographer, James Boswell, tells us that the great man "knew a drum from a trumpet, and a bagpipe from a guitar, which was about the extent of his knowledge of music."

discover, is filled with examples of self-plagiarism. If it was good enough for Handel and Mozart, it should surely be good enough for me.

As usual, I owe a debt of gratitude to numerous librarians for their help in scrounging together the research material for this book. And of course I would have gotten nowhere without the help and talents of Dave Donald, whose illustrations add so much to the text, and Sound And Vision publisher Geoff Savage, who manages somehow to keep all of us more or less afloat. Above all, I'd like to thank my wife, Judy Scott, for her patience, encouragement and computer advice.

DWB
Kingston, August 1990

Preface

My career as a singer didn't exactly have what you might call a typical beginning.

I like all kinds of music, everything from Wagner to pop songs. I remember, as a girl growing up in Montreal, that I spent lots of time with my friends sitting on the fire escape in the evenings singing songs from the radio. (Learning the melodies was easy, but memorizing the words was harder. In those days the publishers used to print all the words as a sort of comic book so you could sing along to Sinatra and everybody else. It's too bad they don't do that anymore.)

Even now I sing all the time, especially when I'm trying to get ready for a performance. Sometimes I hardly even know I'm doing it: people pass me on the street as I'm doing my grocery shopping or something and say under their breath, "There's that woman who hums to herself."

Still, I'm not entirely self-taught: I've had wonderful teachers, even though I've never been to music school.

But if I had gone to music school, this is how I would want to learn about all those composers, by reading David Barber's *When the Fat Lady Sings: Opera History As It Ought To Be Taught.* It's very, very clever, it's a fabulous read, and I wish children who are taught music in school were taught this way.

This is a very humorous book, but at the same time it tells it like it is, or was. David's not really fabricating anything, he just manages to give you the gist of the history while leaving out all the boring bits. It's full of things you can pick up on and talk about at parties, and Dave Donald's drawings are so well done, too.

Don't be put off, by the way, by the title. I think it's darling. These days there are some wonderful and skinny opera singers. But there didn't used to be, especially if they sang Wagner. It comes from eating at too many receptions. (Musical receptions are the funniest things I've ever been to, but that's another story.)

So many lay people feel "music's not for me." But you don't have to study music to enjoy music, or even opera. I've never felt music is an elitist thing, and this book helps prove it.

It would be wonderful to find this book in the seat pockets of airplanes, so that when people arrive in Milan or Rome they'll say, "Let's go to the opera."

When The Fat Lady Sings is so clever that you don't need me to tell you it's clever. You can read it and find out for yourself.

One hopes that the great composers had as much of a sense of humor as David Barber has. I think they might have.

Maureen Forrester, Toronto, 1990

Dedication

This book is dedicated to Thomas Tallis, William Byrd, Johann Sebastian Bach, Johannes Brahms, and all the other great composers who knew better that to write any operas. And to my wife, Judy Scott, who put up with me while I was writing it.

Tutto nel mondo e burla,
l'hom e nato burlone.

(All the world's a joke,
all men are born fools.)

– Giuseppe Verdi, *Falstaff*

Starting A Trend

Have cloud machine, will travel

MONTEVERDI AND CROWD

IF YOU'RE LOOKING FOR SOMEONE to blame for
this whole opera business, look no further than
Claudio Monteverdi (1567-1643), a musician at the court of
Duke Vincenzo Gonzaga of Mantua.

Others may want to place the blame elsewhere (and
there's some pretty strong evidence against Vincenzo Galilei
and his Florentine Camerata gang) but if you ask me,
Monteverdi is the one who should be left holding the bag.
He could have been content to be remembered as one of the
finest composers of madrigals in 17th-century Italy – but
no, that wasn't good enough. He had to go messing around
with a whole new art form. Some composers never learn.

Claudio Zuan Giovanni Antonio Monteverdi was born
in the Italian town of Cremona. His father, Baldasar, like
that of Handel after him, was a barber-surgeon.[1] Cremona
was later to become famous as the home town of the
renowned makers of Stradivarius and Guarnerius violins.
This probably explains why Monteverdi grew up with such
a strong need to fiddle around with the development of
musical forms.

We know nothing about Monteverdi's early musical
training, but he must have picked it up somewhere,

---

[1] Maybe there's a connection here: the reason fewer composers write opera
nowadays is that fewer of them have fathers who are barber-surgeons. Just a
thought. If you were looking for a PhD thesis topic, you might consider it.

3

because he'd written his first book of motets by the time he was 15. When he hit 20, he'd written five books of motets and madrigals, and there was no stopping him.

He got a job as court composer for Duke Vincenzo, who kept him busy writing all sorts of music to keep the duke and his friends entertained. (Vincenzo considered himself the life of the party, and since he was richer than most of his guests they went on letting him think so.)

We don't know very much about Monteverdi the person. He was occasionally hot-tempered and got into arguments with the duke's treasurer about his pay. (Who wouldn't?) He was once robbed by a highwayman, who took all his money but not his cloak, because it was too long. This proves either that Monteverdi was very tall, or that the highwayman was a shrimp. In 1595, Monteverdi married a court singer named Claudia Cattaneo (Claudio and Claudia – how cute!) and they had three children.

In 1600, a music theorist named Giovanni Maria Artusi caused a stir by publishing a treatise attacking modern music. He said there were too many wrong notes and that it all sounded like so much noise. (Sound familiar?) Artusi didn't name any names specifically, but since he cited several examples from the music of Monteverdi, it didn't take a genius to figure out whom he meant.

Monteverdi did the grown-up thing and ignored the insult. He just went ahead and wrote more madrigals. But four years later, Artusi wrote another attack, and this time he wasn't pulling any punches: he came right out and mentioned Monteverdi by name.

That did it: now Monteverdi was really mad. He decided to compose an entirely new form of musical work, one that paid closer attention to the dramatic representation of the words (and one with simpler melodies, so Artusi could follow what was going on). He called it a *favola in musica*, or "story in music", and chose as his story the Greek legend of Orpheus and Eurydice. He called his creation *Orfeo* and it was the first real opera.

A group of musicians led by Vincenzo Galilei (father of

the astronomer Galileo Galilei), who called themselves the Florentine Camarata – or Florentine Gang – had been advocating this form of simplified music drama, the *stile rapprasentativo*, or "representative style," for several years. They thought it was important to get back to the musical ideals established by the ancient Greeks.[2]

This new style of singing was called monody. Don't get that confused with monotony, which is what some of us think opera is really all about.

Two of the Florentine bunch, Jacopo Peri and Giulio Caccini, had even created a little music drama demonstrating their ideas. They composed their *Euridice* in 1601, six years before Monteverdi's version of the same story in 1607. You could argue that the earlier work was the first opera if you want, but it was really just a dry run for the main event. It took a bigshot composer like Monteverdi to really go to town with the new style.[3]

In the original Greek legend, Orpheus travels to the Underworld to rescue his beloved Eurydice from death. The god of the Underworld tells him that Eurydice will follow him back to the land of the living, but that he can't look behind him to check on her. Being the suspicious type, he does anyway, and she dies again – this time for good.

Such a dismal finale would never do for Monteverdi, so he convinced the librettist, Alessandro Striggio, to write him a happy ending. In Monteverdi's *Orfeo*, the god Apollo descends from a marvelous cloud machine, restores Eurydice to life and reunites the happy lovers. (Monteverdi must have liked cloud machines: he used one again in his final opera, *L'Incoronazione di Poppea*. In his opera *Il Ritorno d'Ulisse in Patria*, the god Neptune arrives in the amphibious version, an elaborate sea-machine. "The

---

[2] There was no way they could have known what Greek music sounded like, so they were talking through their hats. But that didn't stop them.

[3] You don't have to take my word for it: Monteverdi, none too modestly, takes the credit for himself.

Florentines," historian Carl Engel remarks tartly in his essay The Beginnings Of Opera, "had more scenery, machinery, and fire-works than was altogether good for them." So there.)

In this, as elsewhere, we can see that Monteverdi was the true pioneer of the operatic art. He established the form, and laid down the principles for many of its lasting conventions. From the very first, Monteverdi's example proved that no matter how ridiculous it made the story, the opera has to have a happy ending.

A Cut Above

Go nuts, castrato

THE CASTRATI LOSE
THEIR MARBLES

THE OPERAS OF MONTEVERDI and other copycat Italians spread through Italy and most of the rest of Europe throughout the mid-17th century. There was no escaping opera. It was everywhere, and every self-respecting city and aristocratic court came to have at least one opera house. (Rich noblemen liked to show off by having two or three, much the same way people today do with cars.)

The late 17th century and the first half of the 18th was the time of what one historian calls the "fullest flowering" of Italian Baroque opera.[1]

Also flowering – vocally, at least, if in no other way – was that singer peculiar to the period – one might even say unique – known as the *castrato*. (In groups, they're called *castrati*. Don't ask me why. That's just the way the Italian language works.)

The castrato got his voice by means of a rather drastic surgical procedure – namely what one writer rather coyly terms "the singular disadvantage of castration." He represents what might be considered the ultimate example of putting art before common sense.

You wanted to be careful in those days in Italy if you were a boy with a beautiful singing voice. If you didn't watch out, you might find that someone had designs on your musical future – designs of which you might not entirely

---

[1] After that, it just went to seed.

9

approve, not that anyone would give you very much choice in the matter. (The practice continued into the next century and spread to other parts of Europe: as a young boy in Vienna, Haydn was once a likely candidate, until his father stepped in and put a stop to the idea. We can presume that Haydn wasn't thrilled with the prospect either.)

The rise, as it were, of the castrati is a subject rather difficult to talk about in polite company, but one nevertheless impossible to avoid in any serious discussion of the history of opera – or even in this one.

It probably happened by accident (someone carelessly stepped on a rake or something), but somewhere along the way it was discovered that castrated boys could develop into remarkable adult singers, with voices that combined the bright clarity of their boyish sound with the muscle and lung power of a grown man. The castrati also came to be known by other, more euphemistic terms, such as *musici* or sometimes *evirati*, which is Italian for "unmanned." (Nowadays the Americans and Soviets talk about "unmanned space probes," but I don't think that's quite the same thing.) Behind their backs, some people called them even worse.

Although eunuchs of one kind or another had been around for a long time, they didn't become popular in musical circles until the 17th century. The first recognized castrati were Pietro Paolo Folignato and Girolamo Rossini, who joined the papal choir in Rome in 1599. (Historian Charles Burney says 1601, but he could be forgetful sometimes.) I'm not sure, by the way, if this Girolamo Rossini is any relation to the later opera composer Gioacchino Rossini, but if they are related it could hardly be through a direct line.

The Vatican developed a curiously hypocritical attitude to the castrati. Officially, castration was not allowed, and anyone found to be performing the operation was sentenced to excommunication. (The proper medical term for complete removal, in case you were wondering, is bilateral orchidectomy, or orchiectomy, or sometimes orchectomy.)

But unofficially, most of the church bigwigs – including

several popes – were ardent opera fans and enjoyed nothing more than listening to the castrati strut their stuff (or what was left of it, anyway). Besides, they needed a steady supply of castrati to sing in the church choirs. (It was their own damn fault: they had this silly notion that women shouldn't be allowed to.)

So they tended to turn a blind eye to the whole routine. Boys were produced who were said to be the victims of unfortunate farming accidents, or of getting mumps at an inconvenient age, or any number of other deceptions. (One castrato in 1800 was said to have been "attacked by a pig." That might do it.)

Women were eventually allowed to sing on the opera stage, but the castrati continued their dominance of the genre. In fact, the whole situation got so ridiculous that at least one young woman, a singer named Teresa Lanti Palesi, spent several years masquerading as a castrato under the name Bellino, just so she could have a perform-ing career. If that doesn't take the cake: a woman pretend-ing to be a man sounding like a woman. (Whenever necessary, historian Angus Heriot tells us in his book The Castrati In Opera, she was able to carry off the deception "with the aid of an instrument which she taped to her body in the appropriate position." He doesn't say what kind of instrument – maybe some kind of flute.)

By 1760 or so, she was able to resume her career under her own name and sex. How do we know all this? Simple. Casanova writes about her in his diary: she was one of his many lovers. I wonder what their pillow talk was like.

At any rate, by the end of the 17th century the whole practice of creating castrati had gotten rather out of hand. By the mid-18th century, an estimated 4,000 boys had gone under the knife – in the 1780s more than 200 in Rome alone, not to mention the other major musical centres of Italy. By one estimate, nearly 70 per cent of all male opera singers in the 18th century were castrati. That's a whole lot of farm accidents.

The worst of it was that it was all a big gamble. Only a small minority of those castrated actually developed into first-rate singers. Most became mediocre at best, while some were no use at all. You might say they just weren't cut out for it.

What to do with the duds became something of an embarrassing problem. Many were allowed to enter the priesthood, though the church had to bend its own rules to allow them in.

It seems that, technically, if a priest's vow of celibacy is to have any merit, the church figures he has to be giving up something that's really worth worrying about. The sophists solved the problem, says the 18th-century German traveller Johann Wilhelm von Archenholz, by deciding that it was "sufficient for such a priest to have his amputated genitals in his pocket, when he approaches the altar." (We shouldn't take this too seriously. There's a chance someone was pulling Archenholz's leg.)

Burney, by the way, thought the whole idea of castrati very barbaric, and states, rather smugly, that the English were far too civilized to allow castration in their country. (They weren't, however, above importing a few Italian castrati to give opera audiences a thrill.) The French disapproved entirely.

In their church music, as well as in opera, the English instead gave high male vocal lines to the counter-tenor, who gets his top notes by training and practice, not surgery. (It's so much less painful that way.) People who don't know any better sometimes think that counter-tenors and castrati are the same thing. But there's a vast difference – or *vas deferens* – between the two.

Burney, at least, was sympathetic. (Among other things, he discounts the rumor that castrati were unable to utter the letter 'r'.) He was also among the first to point out the discrepancy between the official and actual attitudes toward the castrati at the time.

"I enquired throughout Italy," he writes, "at what place boys were chiefly qualified for singing by castration, but could get no certain intelligence. I was told at Milan that it was at Venice; at Venice that it was at Bologna; but at Bologna the fact was denied, and I was referred to Florence;

12

from Florence to Rome; and from Rome I was sent to Naples. The operation is most certainly against the law in all these places, as well as against nature; and all the Italians are so much ashamed of it, that in every province they transfer it to some other." This might be called the 17th-century equivalent of the modern "not-in-my-back-yard" syndrome.

But despite an official ambivalence, the fact remains that the castrati became the most important – I'm tempted to say seminal – singers of Baroque opera (perhaps because they themselves were what you might call Baroque-en). Crowds thrilled to the sound of their voices. Women swooned and had to be carried out of the theatre. ("One God! One Farinelli!" shouted one enthusiastic Englishwoman upon hearing that singer's London debut in 1734.)

Women, in fact, had reason to swoon. Despite a common misconception (pardon the pun), many of the castrati – except maybe the ones who'd been attacked by pigs – remained sexually functional. The surgery that produced the voices by severing the seminal ducts left the rest of the sexual machinery intact. The fact that they couldn't produce children only made them the more attractive as lovers. This was, after all, before the era of safe sex.

Whether they retained the requisite urges is another question entirely. But at least some of them must have: Gaetano Majorano (1710-83), the castrato known as Caffarelli, while carrying on an affair with a certain noblewoman in Rome, narrowly escaped capture when surprised by her husband. Caffarelli had to hide out all night in a disused cistern. He caught a terrible cold, and it serves him right, too. His lover then had to hire a bunch of bodyguards to protect him from the thugs her husband had hired to kill him. Caffarelli eventually gave up and escaped to Venice.

The castrato Consolino found a more devious solution. He carried on a longtime affair with his lover without her husband ever finding out: Consolino would arrive at her house dressed in one of his elaborate stage costumes and her hubby just assumed it was one of her better-dressed lady friends come for a visit.

The castrato Zambinella found a similar situation of mistaken identity rather more inconvenient: the French sculptor Sarassin, Balzac tells us, made advances on Zambinella, thinking the castrato was a woman. This would never do, and eventually, the singer's patron, Cardinal Cicognara, simply had the persistent Frenchman killed. That stopped him.[2]

The best castrati became as famous in their day as any rock superstar of today. They had groupies and adoring fans, they lived like princes and commanded ridiculously large sums of money for their performances. (Sound familiar?)

Some of them were arrogant beyond compare: they thought they were a cut above the competition. Luigi Marchesi, for example, insisted on making his first entrance on horseback, descending from a hill. (It didn't matter if there weren't supposed to be any hills or horses in the opera: if you wanted Marchesi you got him his hill and his horse or he didn't sing.)

Carrying a sword, shield and lance, and wearing a helmet with plumed feathers at least a yard high (I don't know if he brought his own yardstick to measure them with, or what), Marchesi would make his grand entrance singing one of his favorite arias – usually "Mia speranza, io pur vorrei," written especially for him by Giuseppe Sarti.[3]

Caffarelli was not much better. He was once actually thrown in prison, says the official report, for "disturbing the other performers, acting in a manner bordering on lasciviousness with one of the female singers, conversing with the spectators in the boxes, and refusing to sing in the ensembles with the others."

Probably the most famous of the castrati, and certainly one of the least obnoxious, was Carlo Broschi, who was known as Farinelli. (Most of the castrati took stage names

[2] It usually does.

[3] Many singers had such favorite tunes, which came to be known as *arie di baule*, or "suitcase arias," because the singer would carry them with him from performance to performance.

and all of the most famous ones – including Farinelli, Caffarelli, Siface, Senesino and Nicolini – were best known by only a single name, an incompleteness that somehow seems appropriate.)

Farinelli (1705-82) studied in Naples under the famed teacher Niccolo Porpora and went on to perform in numerous Porpora operas. (That's a good tongue-twister: try saying "Porpora operas" quickly, as many times as you can.) His voice was highly regarded for its purity of tone, beauty of sound and agility. (But not everyone was so impressed. The German flutist and composer Johann Joachim Quantz thought that Farinelli's acting – if nothing else – was too stiff.)

After a successful career of more than 15 years (causing an Englishwoman to swoon is no mean feat), Farinelli retired at the tender age of 32 to Spain, where he spent the next decade doing little more than singing for the Spanish king, Philip V.

Philip, it seems, had lapsed into a terrible depression. It was getting embarrassing: he'd stopped shaving and would mope around all day in his bathrobe. His wife Elizabeth, the queen, convinced Farinelli to sing a private concert for the king. It seemed to do the trick: Philip agreed to shave and get dressed and everything. He looked almost human again.

Farinelli's royal gigs became a nightly performance. In fact, if we're to believe Burney, he sang the same four arias every night for nearly ten years. You can believe that if you want, but I like to think that at least every once in a while he threw in something new just to liven up the place.

Farinelli kept busy in other ways, importing Hungarian horses for the king's stables, re-designing the royal opera house to mount lavish productions, and re-directing the course of the River Tagus. (What good's a singer if he can't re-direct a river, I always say.)

Philip kicked the royal bucket in 1746 and was succeeded by Ferdinand VI, whom Farinelli continued to serve until Ferdinand followed suit in 1759. The new king, Charles III, didn't care much for castrati ("Capons are for eating," he once said, rather unkindly, I think) and pensioned Farinelli off to a villa in Bologna, where he spent his final years in luxurious comfort.

By this time the castrati had been toppled from their position as the favorite opera voice, although there were a few remaining over the years. Mozart wrote opera parts for castrato (including one in *La Clemenza di Tito*, interestingly enough, called Sextus). So did Rossini and Meyerbeer. Even Wagner considered transposing the Parsifal role of Klingsor for castrato. Now *that* would have been interesting.[4]

It may be hard to understand nowadays, but the castrati evidently were impressive in their musical delivery. Just listen to 19th-century music historian Enrico Panzacchi:

"What singing! Imagine a voice that combines the sweetness of the flute, and the animated suavity of the human larynx – a voice which leaps and leaps, lightly and spontaneously, like a lark that flies through the air and is intoxicated with its own flight; and when it seems that the voice has reached the loftiest peaks of altitude, it starts off again, leaping and leaping still with equal lightness and equal spontaneity, without the slightest sign of forcing or ..."

Yes. Well. All this leaping is making me dizzy. Let's leave Panzacchi and move on to something a little more down-to-earth.

---

[4] Richard Rodgers and Lorenz Hart, believe it or not, once wrote a Broadway musical based on a book called The Son Of The Grand Eunuch. (Just how the Grand Eunuch could father a son is not quite clear.) It centres on the problems of a young man who has no interest in following in the family business —at least not if it means losing the family jewels. He spends much of the time running around avoiding men with large knives. Towards the end of the second act, when the boy is being taken away for the deed to be done, Rodgers wrote a big triumphal march, into which, just for the heck of it, he threw in a few bars from Tchaikovsky's Nutcracker Suite.

Serious
Buffoonery

Warning: never mix your operatic genres

OPERA SERIA AND OPERA BUFFA

AS THE 18TH CENTURY ROLLED AROUND, opera had wormed its way into the social life of your average everyday aristocrat. Even if you were the Duke of Something-or-other or the Countess Whatnot, you just weren't *anybody* unless you went regularly to the opera.

You didn't have to actually listen to it, mind you, and you certainly didn't have to enjoy it. You just had to be seen to be there. It's pretty much the same today.

Alessandro Scarlatti, a Sicilian boy who later made it big in Naples, had just about cornered the market on Italian opera at the end of the 17th century and through much of the 18th. More than anyone else, Scarlatti popularized the so-called *da capo* aria, in which after performing the first two parts of a song the singer returns to the beginning to sing the opening part again – just in case he didn't get it right the first time around.

Singers loved this routine because it guaranteed them a kind of built-in encore. Some people in the audience appreciated the fact that they could have a second run at trying to understand the words. *Da capo*, which is Italian for "to the head," probably comes from the fact that after singing so many automatic encores, the singers began to think they must be something pretty special. They let their success, in other words, go to their heads.

Scarlatti wrote more than a hundred operas. (He stopped counting after that, and so have I.) It was mostly because of him that the big scene for Italian opera in the early 18th century shifted from Venice to Naples. Everybody wanted to be where the action was. This established what came to be called the Neapolitan school.[1]

As well as the *da capo* aria, Scarlatti made a specialty of something called "the ensemble of perplexity," which is generally how I feel about opera most of the time.

After Scarlatti came such composers as Antonio Caldara, Johann Joseph Fux and Johann Hasse. Fux is best known today, if at all, as the author of *Gradus Ad Parnassum*, that rivetting bestseller that tells you everything you always wanted to know about counterpoint (but were afraid to ask).[2] Hasse was married to Faustina Bordoni, a famous operatic soprano who had a habit of getting into fights on stage. I can only imagine what their home life must have been like.

The most famous librettist of the day was born Antonio Domenico Bonaventura Trapassi. As a small boy he was adopted by a judge named Gian Vincenzo Gravina, who for some reason changed the boy's name to Pietro Metastasio. Well, it made sense to *him*.

Metastasio's adopted father wanted his boy to become a lawyer, but when Daddy died and left him a small fortune, Metastasio chucked the idea of law school and decided to devote himself to becoming a poet. It just seemed easier.

He'd already shown himself to be quick-witted with little improvised verses (you know, "There was a young girl from Nantucket" – that sort of thing) and before you knew it, Metastasio was writing opera libretti and ceremonial poetry for the Holy Roman Emperor Charles VI.

Metastasio wrote nearly 30 operas – or more than 70, depending on who's counting. Most of them are in three acts, as opposed to the five-act format everyone had been writing until he came along. This would have been more of an improvement except his three-act operas were just as

---

[1] Some people think that Neapolitan opera, like the ice cream, comes in three flavors: chocolate, strawberry and vanilla. I wish they were right.

[2] Counterpoint is a kind of musical needlepoint, made famous by J.S. Bach as a means of proving how intellectually inadequate all the rest of us are.

long as the earlier five-act ones, so we're really no further ahead.

Just about everybody who was anybody – and a few who were nobodies – took a stab at setting a Metastasio opera, from Albinoni to Vivaldi to Hasse to Handel to Porpora to J.C. Bach to Mozart. There are nearly 1,000 opera settings of Metastasio texts, so needless to say there's a bit of duplication here and there. You could hardly avoid it.

All of Metastasio's librettos tell the same kind of story. The hero or heroine is someone impossibly noble struggling with a difficult choice between love and duty. There was often some sort of mistaken identity in there just to make things more interesting, and eventually everything resolves itself into a kind of happy ending – but not before the singers have spent a few hours of long-winded agonizing in full voice (while the audience agonizes in comparative silence).

This form of highbrow entertainment came to be known as *opera seria,* because it was serious stuff. "The *opera seria* libretto," the latest edition of Grove's dictionary tells us, "originated in the Arcadian neo-classical reform of Italian libretto of the late 17th century." Now you know.

After a while, operagoers began finding that the problem with *opera seria* was that it was just so, well, *serious.* All that hand-wringing and all that nobility of character got to be a bit much. The plots were so complicated that singers had to spend great chunks of time singing *recitative* just to get over all the text so they could get on with singing their big arias. The end result of this was to make the singers a more important element. This is never a wise move.

With all this heavy-duty emoting happening on stage, audiences grew restless. And probably the composers did, too. What they needed was to have a little fun. As the big operas grew more and more serious, composers began writing little funny scenes to insert between the acts. These bits of comic relief, which often played in front of the curtain while the stagehands shifted scenery behind, came to be known as *intermezzi.* Pretty soon they started getting longer too, and came to be known as *opera buffa*, or "comic opera."

Opera buffa does not mean, as you might think, opera in the nude. There are laws against that sort of thing.

"Comic opera," historian Donald Jay Grout tells us with his usual knack of hitting the nail on the head, "sheds a ray of sunshine over an otherwise distressingly humorless landscape." Well, something had to be done or we'd have all died of terminal angst.

Unlike *opera seria*, which is all about aristocrats and gods and important bigwigs, *opera buffa* was usually about servants and peasants and ordinary common folk. (If there were noblemen in *opera buffa*, they were usually there to be made fun of.)

No study of *opera buffa* would be complete without a mention of the most famous one, *La serva padrona*, or The Maid As Mistress, by the Italian composer Giovanni Battista Draghi Pergolesi. This wasn't the first opera buffa – in fact, it wasn't really an *opera buffa* at all but just an *intermezzo*. But it's the one that always gets mentioned, so who am I to buck a trend?

La serva padrona made its debut in Naples in 1733, wedged in between the acts of a far more serious and now totally forgotten opera called *Il prigionier superbo*, or The Proud Prisoner.[3] Pergolesi's simple little ditty tells the story of how a wealthy bachelor, Uberto, is happily duped into marrying his maid, Serpina. The only other character in the story is Uberto's valet, Vespone, a mute role in which the performer neither sings nor speaks. Operas should have a lot more roles like this one.

The story opens with Uberto complaining that Serpina has not brought him his morning cup of hot chocolate. She comes in to tell him to get his own drinks and that furthermore he should get married. (She's a bit more subtle in setting it up, but that's the gist of it.)

---

[3] An opera now so totally forgotten that I can't even tell you who wrote it. That's fame for you.

That's the first part. In the second part, Serpina disguises Vespone as a dashing captain to make Uberto jealous enough to propose to her. It works. The music ends with a charming little love duet, giving the story a happy ending – except that Uberto never does get his hot chocolate.

Pergolesi's tunes are catchy, if not terribly profound. But even though his music sounds a bit like watered-down Mozart, we shouldn't under-estimate the importance of Pergolesi's contribution to the development of opera. If it weren't for him, there might not have been any *opera buffa* or any of the later comic operas. We'd have none of the funny operas of Mozart but only the deadly serious ones of Wagner. I shudder to think. (Unfortunately, Pergolesi's best efforts weren't enough to stop Wagner completely, but at least he tried.)

Before his sudden death in 1736 at the age of 26, Pergolesi's works, as one historian puts it, "brought fresh air to opera." I guess all that breathing must have been too much for him: he died of tuberculosis.

French Bred

Lully was radiant as the Sun King of French opera

LULLY, RAMEAU
AND GLUCK

THE FRENCH, BEING FRENCH, didn't pay much attention to what went on in the rest of the operatic world. They wanted to go their own way and they didn't care who knew it. This is known as the Gallic temperament.

French audiences, had begun the 17th century with the usual imported productions of Italian opera, since that was the only game in town. But pretty soon there was a move afoot for composers to write operas that were distinctly French. They'd had enough of these foreign imports.

The first sure-fire way to do this, obviously, was to use a French text by a French playwright. The other guaranteed trick was to throw in some extra dancing: there's nothing a 17th-century French audience seemed to like more than a little gratuitous ballet.

It's ironic, considering how strongly the French were feeling, that two of the most important composers in the development of French opera in the 17th and 18th centuries weren't Frenchmen at all. The first, Jean-Baptiste Lully, was really an Italian. The other, Christoph Willibald Gluck, was one of those Europeans it's hard to pin down, but who was more Austrian than anything else. Just one of life's little jokes, I guess.

Lully was born in Florence in 1632 and named Giovanni Battista Lulli. He liked to tell people he was descended from nobility but don't you believe a word of it: his father, Lorenzo Lulli, was a miller and his mother, Caterina di Gabriello del Serva, was a miller's daughter. Perfectly respectable, but hardly noble.

As a boy, young Lully was shipped off to Paris to serve as *valet de chambre* for Mademoiselle de Montpensier, the king's cousin. Pretty soon he found himself performing in the court orchestra of the king himself. Not long after that he was writing ballet music for plays by Moliere and found himself appointed court composer.

By 1672 he'd got himself named director of the Academie Royale de Musique and began writing operas. It's probably better if you don't ask how he managed to get the job.[1]

Lully's first opera was *Cadmus et Hermione* in 1673, followed by about 20 others over the next 14 years, all of them based on classical Greek myths as adapted by his librettist, Philippe Quinault. (Lully's melodies, one historian tells us, were perfectly matched to "the swelling, rolling lines of Quinault's poetry." A lesser composer might have become seasick.)

Lully's operas follow a predictable pattern. They begin with an overture (known as a "French" overture, to distinguish it from the "Italian" overture developed by Scarlatti). French overtures start with a slow, pompous introduction with a typically dotted rhythm, followed by a faster imitative middle section and ending with a slowish dance section. (Italian overtures go fast-slow-fast instead of slow-fast-slow, just so you know.)

After the overture came a pastoral prologue, with just a little bit of dancing to whet the appetite, in which the characters lounge around saying what a wonderful guy the king is. This is known as earning brownie points. After that, Lully launched into the five-act tragedy, broken up now and then by dance movements just to keep the *corps du ballet* busy (and on their toes).

Lully was a hard worker but he could have fun when he wanted to. Once, during a performance in 1681 of *Le Bourgeois gentilhomme* in which Lully was acting, he took

---

[1] Let's just say a lot of money changed hands.

a flying leap and landed on the harpsichord in the pit, smashing it to bits just to make the king laugh. For this the king appointed him *secretaire du roi.*[2]

He also knew how to party. For a performance of his opera *Persee* at the royal palace in 1682, he arranged to have a huge arch constructed with fountains that spouted wine all night. (What the hell, he probably wasn't the one paying for it.)

Lully came to a bizarre end in 1687 by dying of a stubbed toe. This happened during a performance of his *Te Deum* to celebrate the king's recovery from surgery.[3]

Before conductors began using those elegant white batons, it was the custom in those days to beat time on the floor with a big, heavy stick. Unfortunately Lully wasn't paying attention and bashed himself on the foot. He later developed gangrene and died from blood poisoning. (A friend had paid the Marquis de Cavette 2,000 pistoles to cure Lully. But the marquis was a complete quack, so it was just money down the drain.)

After Lully, the mantle of French opera passed on to Jean-Philippe Rameau, a true Frenchman born in 1683 in Dijon, where the mustard comes from. Rameau was an accomplished harpsichord player and theorist who wrote a treatise on harmony in 1722 that's still considered impor-tant today – but only if you like that sort of thing.

As a young man he travelled to Italy but wasn't much impressed by the operas he saw there. By 1705 he was back in Paris as a musician for Le Riche de la Pouplinaire, a local bigwig.

Rameau wrote his first opera, *Hippolyte et Aricie*, in 1733, followed by what he called a ballet-opera (not to be confused with a ballad opera), *Les Indes galantes*, in 1735.

[2] The chief duty of a *secretaire du roi*, apparently, was to make sure the king had enough money on hand for going to war or buying his mistress a new dress.

[3] The nature of the surgery, to remove a rectal abscess, was rarely mentioned in polite company.

He wrote his most famous opera, *Castor et Pollux*, in 1737.[4]

Castor et Pollux tells the story of a couple of twin brothers named, naturally enough, Castor and Pollux. Their mother was Leda and their father was Zeus during one of his swan phases. They had a couple of twin sisters named Helen and Clytemnestra.

Everything is going along swimmingly until one day Castor is killed by Idas for killing Idas's twin brother Lynceus. (There are just too many twins in this story.) Hearing of the death of Castor, as one historian puts it, "Pollux is beside himself with grief."[5]

In a variation of the old Orpheus story, Pollux appeals to the gods to let him trade places with his brother in the Underworld. (No, not with the gangsters: the *other* Underworld.) Zeus, impressed by his devotion, agrees to turn the both of them into the constellation we now call Gemini, or The Twins. This isn't exactly what Pollux had in mind, but it makes him happy anyway.[6]

Rameau's career might have been pleasantly unremarkable if it weren't for a scandal that came to be known as "*la guerre des bouffons*," or "the War of the Buffoonists."

This began in 1752 when a touring Italian troupe brought a production of Pergolesi's *La serva padrona* to Paris.[7] This prompted Jean-Jacques Rousseau, that well-known philosopher and troublemaker, to declare that Rameau's operas were dull and boring and not nearly as good as the Italian *opera buffa*.

Rousseau had some pretty important followers, including the Queen. But Rameau's supporters included the King and his mistress, Madame de Pompadour, as well as the philosopher and all-around wit Voltaire. They stuck by

---

[4] It's probably just coincidence that so many French operas sound like the names of law firms.

[5] It's easier to be beside yourself when you have a twin brother.

[6] Nowadays if someone in opera circles says "I'm going to turn you into a star" it usually means something different.

[7] Anybody who doesn't remember about *La serva padrona* should go back one chapter and read it again.

him despite his personal faults: he could be mean, boorish and insulting, but he knew how to write music.[8]

The battle lines were quickly drawn for the same sort of high-society intellectual dispute that later flared up around Gluck and in London with the Handel/Bononcini rivalry. There's nothing opera lovers like more than a good fight among snobs.

The Rameau camp scored a sneaky victory with a production of a supposed Italian *opera buffa* that turned out to have been written by a French composer, thus proving that the French could be fun when they wanted to be. This led to the development of the *opera-comique*, the French equivalent of the Italian *opera buffa.* The buffoon-ists' camp eventually had to admit defeat, although a few of them stuck around long enough to make trouble for Gluck. Rameau ended his part of the dispute by dying of typhoid fever in 1764. He'd had enough already.

The next big figure in French opera is Gluck, a for-ester's son who was born in 1714 in Erasbach, which in those days was more or less part of Bohemia. He was the oldest of nine kids: his parents called him Christoph Willibald so they wouldn't confuse him with his brother Christoph Anton.[9]

As a young man he got a job in Vienna, playing in the orchestra of Prince Lobkowitz, and then went off to Italy to write a bunch of operas on librettos written, like everyone else's, by Metastasio. Then he returned to Vienna and did more of the same.

In 1750 he married Maria Anna Bergin (or Pergin), the daughter of a wealthy Viennese banker and merchant. Since Daddy didn't approve of Gluck marrying his little girl, they'd had to wait until he died to go through with the

---

[8] Voltaire had written librettos for several Rameau operas, so he had what you'd call a vested interest.

[9] Others got confused over his name, too. His marriage licence spells his last name Gluckh, and he signed it Christopf. His friend Marianne Pirker, wife of the violinist Franz Joseph Pirker, refers to him as Cluch and Klug at two different times in one letter.

wedding. Her fortune helped Gluck through the lean years.

Later on he was granted a knighthood by Pope Benedict XIV and after that he insisted on being called Ritter von Gluck or Chevalier Gluck. (In England, he'd have been Sir Christopher.)

Gluck's first 35 or so operas are pretty ordinary, even for *opera seria*. There's *Cleonice and Demofoonte* and *Sofonisba* and a whole slew of others, including a version of *La Clemenza di Tito* written five years before Mozart was even born.

It wasn't until 1762 that Gluck came up with an opera that knocked everyone's socks off. By this time he'd decided that Italian opera had grown "wearisome and ridiculous" and was overburdened by a "useless superfluity of ornaments."[10] What it needed, he said, was a good, thorough housecleaning.

To do this he composed *Orfeo et Euridice*, using a new version by Ranieri da Calzabigi of the same old Orpheus legend with which Monteverdi had opened the whole can of worms in the first place.

Other than using a castrato in the leading male role, there was little about Gluck's opera that wasn't refreshingly new. The music is simple yet elegant, the action clear and uncluttered by extravagant special effects. In arias such as Orpheus's beautiful "Che faro senza Euridice" Gluck manages to avoid all the overblown vocal acrobatics for which opera singers had become famous.

His next opera, *Alceste*, goes even further. It has an overture that actually has something to do with the music of the opera (instead of merely providing background noise for the audience members to settle in their seats) and it assigns the leading male role to a tenor instead of a castrato.

Gluck's snobby Viennese audiences were not ready for such big-league changes, so he went off to Paris to try his luck there.

---

[10] He should know. He'd written enough of them himself.

The French were more receptive to his ideas, if only because it was a way to put the Italians in their place. Queen Marie Antoinette, who'd been his singing pupil in Vienna, gave the nod to Gluck's *Iphegenie en Aulide* in 1774 and to a revival that year of *Orfeo* with a tenor replacing the castrato lead.

But not everyone was happy. There was still a strong faction of Italian diehards, who imported Niccolo Piccinni (not to be confused with Giacomo Puccini) to square off against the upstart reformer.

The rivalry created by the followers of the two composers was pretty much like all the others: either you were a Gluckist or a Piccinnist and there were no two ways about it. (For their part, Gluck and Piccinni thought the whole thing was pretty silly, though it was good for business. They remained friendly through most of the hubbub.)

Eventually the director of the Academie Royale de Musique, knowing a good marketing ploy when he saw one, commissioned each composer to write an opera based on the same story by Euripides. Gluck's version is *Iphegenie en Tauride*, a sequel to his earlier *Iphegenie en Aulide*.[11]

Gluck's version of 1779 was a much greater success that Piccinni's – partly because Piccinni's soprano was falling down drunk on the opening night. This never helps.

Gluck's last opera, *Echo et Narcisse*, was less popular, but by then his success was assured. He moved to Vienna, where he spent his retirement. Gloating.

---

[11] If Gluck were writing movies nowadays, he'd have called it Iphegenia II.

Being bullish on Carmen

BIZET

BIZET NEVER INTENDED TO BE a one-opera wonder. It just worked out that way.

Actually, he did compose more than one opera, but it's
largely for *Carmen* that he's remembered today. He believed in saving the best till the last.

Bizet was born in Paris in 1838 to a musical family. His
father, Adolphe, was a singing teacher. His mother, Aimée,
played the piano quite well. They named their boy Alex-
andre-César Léopold Bizet, but everybody called him
Georges.[1]

All of Bizet's early life – the piano lessons, the lessons
at the Conservatoire, the prizes he won, his impressive
Symphony in C major – suggest he should have had it made
as a big-time composer. But he spent a lot of time slogging
away at hack-work, writing piano arrangements of operas
by other composers.[2]

Nevertheless he did find time to write some of his own
music, including the operas *Le Docteur Miracle*, *Don Pro-
copio*, and his only pre-*Carmen* success, *Les Pecheurs de
perles* (The Pearl Fishers), which contains the famous
tenor-baritone duet "Au fond du temple saint."

He tried several times to write other operas, too. Some,
such as *L'Amour peintre* and *Ivan IV*, are incomplete.

---

[1] This confuses some people, who think his name must somehow be plural.
But there's only one Georges.

[2] He was also a music critic for a while, writing under the pen name Gaston
de Betzi, an anagram of his own surname.

Others, such as *Don Quichotte* and *Griséledis*, he only talked about writing. He had trouble getting around to things.

Bizet's long-awaited success came in 1875 with the Paris premiere of *Carmen*, a story of passionate love, jealousy and cigarette smuggling. Among the hit songs in this opera are the famous Toreador Song and Carmen's seductive Habanera (the melody of which Bizet stole from the Spanish composer Sebastian Yradier, without so much as a by-your-leave).

Carmen opens in a town square in Seville, where the soldier Don José sees a woman coming out from a nearby cigarette factory. She is the gypsy Carmen, who dances sexily and sings the Habanera. He pretends to ignore her but we know he's been hooked.

Then Carmen starts a fight with another of the factory workers (over stolen cigarettes or something) and Don Jose's boss orders him to arrest her. But she bats her dark eyes at him and she manages to escape, whereupon he is jailed as an accomplice.

Anyway, things go from bad to worse – a decline hastened by the braggart Escamillo singing his pushy Toreador Song – and eventually Don Jose ends up in thick with Carmen and a bunch of cigarette smugglers. (They open Act III belting out a chorus about how quiet they have to be as smugglers. It's a wonder they don't wake the neighborhood.)[3]

By this time Carmen has grown tired of Don Jose.[4] She calls him a mama's boy and tells him to take a hike, saying she'd rather hang around with Escamillo. The bullfighter may be arrogant, but at least he's rich.

In Act IV, Don Jose confronts Carmen and, in a fit of jealous rage, stabs her so suddenly she doesn't even get time to sing a dying aria.

Her death makes it unnecessary for the opera to have an Act V and proves once and for all what doctors have been telling us for years: cigarettes can be hazardous to your health, especially if you're a singer.

[3] Or the audience.
[4] I'm surprised she's able to last even that long.

The English Channel

Handel works up an appetite as Giulio Cesare in Egypt

HANDEL

HANDEL WAS BORN IN GERMANY and wrote operas in Italian, so he's considered among the greatest of England's composers. Life's funny that way.

If you wanted to be really picky you might point out that Handel wasn't actually born in Germany, but in a part of Saxony. But it was all part of the Germanic empire, so let's not quibble. Call Handel a Saxon composer nowadays and people look at you funny.

He was born in the Saxon town of Halle in a house known as *Zum gelben Hirsch*, or The Yellow Stag, which had once been a tavern. His father had a running argument with the town council about keeping the liquor licence. He eventually won the fight by appealing to the elector, who threatened to call in the troops. This proves you *can* fight City Hall, but it helps to know the right people.

On that same street in the town today is a house decorated with fancy garlands, a bust of the composer, elaborately carved scrollwork showing the names of the composer's famous oratorios and a plaque that says "Handel's birthplace." He wasn't born there: he was born in the house next door.

Handel was born on February 23rd, 1685, the same year as that other big-name Baroque composer, Johann Sebastian Bach. Even at the best of times Handel was the more famous one: his operas and other stuff earned him an international reputation, enough that Bach spent some time studying some of his early works. Handel, on the other hand, had never even heard of Bach. If he had, Handel probably would have dismissed the other composer as a somewhat talented, though pedantic, church organist. Boy, was *he* in for a surprise.

The two of them never met, but today they are together considered the greatest composers of their generation. People like to argue over who was better, but if you ask me Bach beats out Handel hands down, if only because Bach never composed any operas. Now *that's* what I call greatness.

Handel wasn't that much of a bigwig when he was born. He was, after all, just another baby. But his father, Georg, was something of a local celebrity, having been appointed barber-surgeon to the Elector of Brandenburg.[1]

You don't hear much about barber-surgeons these days: school guidance counsellors would probably discourage you from wanting to study that sort of combined major. But in 17th-century Europe it was a perfectly respectable trade. In fact, Handel's father is described in the register of his second marriage (to Handel's mother, Dorothea Taust, a pastor's daughter of Giebichenstein) as "noble, honorable, greatly respected and renowned," which gives you some idea of how important he must have been. He was past 60 when Handel was born, so he'd had a while to build up his reputation. Considering he'd started out as the elector's valet, he'd done pretty well for himself.

The baptismal certificate gives the newborn composer's name as Georg Friederich Händel, but when he got to England he liked to call himself George Frideric Handel.

Life would be a whole lot easier if he'd gone all the way in Anglicizing his given names to George Frederick. But he liked Frideric, so what can you do? (The confusion over his name existed throughout his life: you'll find it given as Händel, Handel, Handell, Hendell, Hendel, Handl, Hendal, Hendle, Hendall and probably a few more I haven't discovered. Anyway, they're all the same guy. You just had to be

[1] Handel missed his chance as a boy: any music he wrote for his dad's boss might now be known as Brandenburg concertos. But Bach beat him to it.

40

careful if he owed you money.)

Old Georg was a sourpuss who dressed in black all the time and wanted his boy to become a lawyer – but, like Metastasio before him, Handel had other plans. After working for a few years as an organist, the 18-year-old Handel set off to make his fortune writing operas in the big city of Hamburg. There he met Johann Mattheson, a fellow composer a few years older. They became friends, although their friendship was not without its rough moments.

Their most famous argument came in December, 1704, at a performance of Mattheson's opera *Cleopatra*. Mattheson was conducting the performance as well as singing the role of Anthony. (Handel's first biographer, John Mainwaring, was of the opinion that Mattheson "was no great singer.") When he wasn't on stage as Anthony, Mattheson would play harpsichord in the orchestra pit. When he was on stage, Handel would play harpsichord instead of second violin. Anthony kills himself about a half-hour from the end of the show, so Mattheson would always return to the keyboard to play the last part, and naturally to bask in the audience's final applause.

It seems that on this particular night Handel decided he was having too much fun to relinquish the keyboard spot to Mattheson, who promptly called him a variety of rude names – which always sound even worse in German – and challenged him to a duel.

The duel didn't last very long: Mattheson's sword hit one of the buttons on Handel's coat and broke off in his hand. They stayed friends after that, but Handel probably made sure the buttons on his coats were always firmly sewn on.[2]

Handel's first two operas were produced in Hamburg in 1705, *Almira* and *Florindo*. (Displaying his typical sense of economy, Handel later split *Florindo* into two operas, *Florindo* and *Daphne*.) These weren't much more than

[2] In later years they grew apart again. To hear Mattheson tell it, he taught Handel everything he knew.

practice runs, and except for the bits he stole from them to use over again, you probably won't have heard them.[3]

Hoping for bigger fame, Handel set off for Italy, arriving in Florence and later in Rome. But his timing was bad: Pope Clement XI had just slapped a ban on opera. It was something he did every once in a while, just to show that he could. (He was probably in a snit from having backed the losing team in the War of the Spanish Succession.)[4]

Handel's Roman holiday was not a complete washout. He kept himself busy composing concertos and cantatas and generally rubbing elbows with the rich and famous. He acquired himself a generous noble patron, the prince Francesco Maria Ruspoli, (and, rumor has it, a mistress or two), and managed to get his opera *Rodrigo* performed in Florence.

But soon he was off to Venice, where he mounted a production of his opera *Agrippina*. Handel, always a great borrower, used for *Agrippina* some of the music he'd written for *Rodrigo* and *Almira*. Well there was no point letting good tunes go to waste.[5]

The Venetian audiences loved *Agrippina*. Handel was a big hit. One of the people who sat through the whole run of 27 performances was Prince Ernest of Hanover, who immediately offered Handel a job as court musician to his daddy, the Elector of Hanover. It seemed like a good deal, so in 1710 Handel took it and went home to Germany.

Handel hadn't been at his new job very long before he got itchy feet and wanted to go off to England. There he composed his opera *Rinaldo,* which took him only about two weeks to write because he used a lot of the music he'd written for *Agrippina*. He figured the London audiences

---

[3] You're not missing much: they sound like all his later ones anyway, only not so much so.

[4] Clement XI wasn't nearly so drastic as some of his predecessors. In 1697, Pope Innocent XI had ordered an opera house burned to the ground.

[5] Handel often used his own music over again. It saved time. Sometimes he got a little carried away and borrowed from other composers, too.

wouldn't recognize it. He was right.[6]

The plot of *Rinaldo* – which Gluck later used in *Armide*, by the way – takes place during the first Crusade and tells of a love affair between the queen Armida and Rinaldo, the leader of the crusaders. When he dumps her to go off to war she burns down her palace – either out of grief or to get the insurance money, I'm not sure which.

Anyway, the London audiences loved *Rinaldo*, advertised as being composed by "Georgio Frederico Hendel." They especially liked the hit arias "Care sposa" and "Lascia ch'io pianga." The opening march became the regimental theme song of the London Life Guards.

There's a scene towards the end of the first act where the heroine, Almirena, sings to a bunch of birds. That first London production of the opera used real birds at this point, with a stagehand releasing sparrows onto the stage. Nobody does this nowadays. It's too much trouble (and the sparrows are probably all unionized).

Feeling a little guilty after a seven-month stay in England, Handel returned to his job in Hanover, just long enough to compose a slew of songs and some chamber music.

But that music just didn't have the glamorous appeal that came from writing operas, so pretty soon Handel asked permission again to visit England.

He left for England in 1712, having promised the elector he would return to Hanover "within a reasonable time." His second London "visit" lasted nearly 50 years, until his death in 1759. His promise to the elector, Mainwaring tells us, "somehow slipt out of his memory." Happens to the best of us, I guess.

As it turned out, the elector didn't have much to lose. When Queen Anne died in 1714 he became King George I of England and more or less got Handel back again by default as a court composer. George got the crown even

---

[6] It only confused matters that an advertisement in the London Daily Courant gave the opera's title as *Binaldo*. That's newspaper advertising for you.

though he hardly spoke a word of English, which you'd think would be one of the job requirements. Anyway, he stood around muttering in German and people tried not to notice.

On returning to England, Handel set about churning out one opera after another: *Il pastor fido*, *Teseo*, *Silla*, *Amadigi di Gaula* and revivals of some of his earlier ones. He was on a roll. (His theatre manager, meanwhile, was on the lam. After the second night of *Teseo* in January, 1713, Owen Swiney skipped town with the box-office receipts, leaving Handel and his company unpaid. Swiney went to Italy, but returned to England some 20 years later, having changed his name to MacSwiney. Wouldn't you?)

After the sudden departure of Owen Swiney, the management of the Queen's Theatre, where Handel's operas were being performed, was taken over by the Swiss-born assistant manager, Johann Jacob Heidegger, also known as John Jacob (or J.J. to his friends). Heidegger was incredibly efficient and, more to the point, trustworthy. His partnership with Handel was a long and profitable one. Mary Granville, who later became good friends with Handel, once called Heidegger "the most ugly man that was ever formed." But she was only 10 years old at the time and so hadn't yet learned tact.

Not that Handel himself was a model of tact, mind you. He tended to be gruff, demanding and impatient: any singer who threw a tantrum soon found a ready match. In one famous anecdote (so famous that I've already told it in my book *Bach, Beethoven, And The Boys*), the soprano Francesca Cuzzoni refused to sing the aria "Falsa imagine," from Handel's opera *Ottone*, the way the composer wanted. Handel ended their brief shouting match by picking her up and holding her out the window. Then she saw things his way.[7]

Cuzzoni was one of Handel's chief singers in the 1720s

---

[7] Some versions of this story say he only threatened to put her out the window, but I like this one better.

and '30s, after a bunch of high mucky-mucks got together to form the Royal Academy of Music to produce operas and they asked Handel to be the music director. The venture was called the Royal Academy because most of its charter members were earls and dukes and because George I had given it his blessing.[8]

George I didn't know much about music but he liked going to the opera just for the fun of it. He'd sit in the royal box and tell jokes to his mistresses. (Quite aside from his wife the queen, George had two principal mistresses, one of whom was very fat and the other very skinny. The plumpish one was Charlotte Sophia Kelmanns, whom some people said was his half-sister. He generally preferred the skinny one, Ehrengard Melusina von Schulenberg, whom he made the Duchess of Kendall. It was all very innocent, really: they'd sit in her apartment and cut out paper dolls till all hours of the morning.)[9]

The Royal Academy began producing operas at a new theatre in the Haymarket, for which Heidegger handled the business, Handel wrote the music and an Italian named Paolo Rolli wrote most of the librettos. Rolli treated Handel with barely concealed contempt: in his letters he refers to the composer, in a variety of languages, as "the Alpine Faun," "the Bear," "the Savage" and a few more names that are even less flattering and difficult to translate.[10]

All told, Handel composed some 42 operas (I'm not counting *Muzio Scevola*, a combined effort for which he wrote only the third act). Ten of them, or nearly 25 per cent, have titles beginning with the letter A, including *Admato*, *Agrippina*, *Alessandro* and seven others. *Radimisto*, *Rinaldo* and three others begin with R, and five also begin

[8] One of the founders was named George Harrison. Who says the Beatles have no class?

[9] The royal family seemed to have a relaxed attitude about mistresses. When George's successor, George II, took as his mistress Lady Henrietta Howard, his wife allowed that it probably would improve his English.

[10] Rolli didn't limit his comments to Handel: he usually referred to the singer Margarita Duristanti as "the Elephant."

with S. There are four Fs, three each of G, I and P, two Ds, two Os and one each of B, E, I, L and N. I have no idea what, if anything, this proves. But I thought it might interest you to know in case anyone asks.

The operas Handel wrote for the Haymarket theatre were almost all your basic *opera seria* types, with larger-than-life historical figures doing impossible things in the heroic leading roles. Most of the male leads went to a famous Italian castrato named Francesco Bernardi, better known as Senesino. His Handel performances included roles in *Tamerlano*, *Giulio Cesare in Egitto*, *Rodelinda* (where he sang the popular aria "Dove sei, amato bene?") *Tolomeo* and *Serse*, (where he sang the aria "Ombra mai fu," now known as the famous "Largo." It opens the show with Xerxes singing to a shade tree. I guess it takes all kinds.)

Like many or even most of the famous castrati of his day, Senesino was haughty, arrogant and not nearly so wonderful as he thought he was. In the 1732 production of *Giulio Cesare*, Senesino had just heroically declaimed the phrase *"Cesare non seppe mai, che sia timore"* ("Caesar does not know what fear is") when a piece of scenery fell down beside him. He promptly threw himself onto the stage and burst into tears.[11]

The other principal singer of Handel's Academy days was the mezzo-soprano Faustina Bordoni, known as Faustina, whose rivalry with Cuzzoni became legendary.

Her arrival in England from Italy in 1726 put Cuzzoni's nose out of joint.[12] Handel managed to appease the two singers somewhat by writing *Alessandro*, an opera in which the two leading female parts are so carefully balanced that neither is more important than the other. He even went so far as to count out the number of notes.

The Cuzzoni-Faustina rivalry finally blew up in 1727,

---

[11] The absence of castrati is one of the chief reasons that Handel operas are performed so rarely these days. If they were all like Senesino I'm not sure that's such a bad thing.

[12] You wanted to be careful not to anger Cuzzoni: rumor had it she'd poisoned one of her husbands.

during a production of Giovanni Battista Bononcini's opera *Astianate*. Members of the audience had been cheering or booing their favorite of the two singers each time one or the other appeared, to the point where you could hardly hear the singing for all the commotion. Pretty soon a fight broke out in the crowd, followed by one on stage, with the two singers clawing and scratching at each other like a regular cat fight. It was not what you might call professional decorum.

Handel was having similar problems of his own around this time. There was an ongoing rivalry with Bononcini, who was named co-director of music for the Royal Academy, and later on a rivalry with another composer, Niccolo Porpora, who in his earlier years as a teacher had instructed both Senesino and Farinelli.

Porpora came to London in 1729 and in 1733 established the so-called Opera of the Nobility at the request of Frederick, the Prince of Wales.[13] The prince wanted to remove Handel from the opera scene in favor of Porpora. This had less to do with the composers than it did with the feud between the prince and his daddy the king. Handel and Porpora were just kind of caught in the middle.

The real threat to Handel's career came from a musical production in 1728 called *The Beggar's Opera*, with music by Johann Pepusch and lyrics by John Gay. Other than the overture, Pepusch didn't actually compose much of the music for what they called their ballad opera. All he did was arrange the stolen opera arias and folk songs that made up the score. This, of course, saved time.

The Beggar's Opera opened on January 29 and had a run of 63 performances, which is more than Handel ever managed with any of his operas. People liked the ballad opera because it was satirical, funny and easy to understand, since the songs were in English.

[13] George I had died in 1727 and been succeeded by the previous Prince of Wales, George Augustus, who became George II. Nobody noticed much difference, except George II's english was a bit easier to understand.

There hadn't been much opera in English before this. Henry Purcell made his one great contribution to the genre with *Dido and Aeneas*, written for a girls' boarding school in 1689, and which contains the famous aria "When I am laid in earth," known as "Dido's lament." But Purcell got busy with other things and then died quite suddenly in 1695 without having written another opera. This proves the danger of procrastination: I'm sure he'd always meant to write a few more when he could find the time.

Be that as it may, the point is that the English were growing tired of having to rely on foreigners for their operas, so when the Gay/Pepusch ballad opera came along, it found a large and willing audience. As if it weren't bad enough that the great German composer was being supplanted, to add insult to injury two of the musical numbers in *The Beggar's Opera* were stolen from Handel himself, including an aria and the march from *Rinaldo*.

Other ballad operas by Gay and Pepusch and by others soon followed, including *The Wedding*, *Polly*, *The Quaker's Opera* and *The Female Parson*. The crowds loved them.[14]

Handel hung in there writing serious Italian operas for another 10 years, but his heart wasn't really in it. He could see the writing on the wall: his opera career was coming to a close.

As early as 1732 he began hedging his bets by composing *Esther*, the first oratorio. A Handel oratorio is not much different from a Handel opera: he uses the same mixture of arias and recitatives to tell the story. But instead of Greek and Roman histories, oratorios relate a story from the Bible. There's often just as much violence and bloodshed, but telling it in a Biblical context is supposed to make it somehow more uplifting.

The big difference, of course, is that oratorios don't require stage sets or costumes, making them considerably

---

[14] Bertolt Brecht and Kurt Weill later revised *The Beggar's Opera* in German and called it *The Threepenny Opera*, from which we get the great jazz tune "Mack The Knife."

cheaper to produce. Think of oratorio as opera performed on the radio.

Handel's most famous oratorio, of course, is *Messiah*, which he wrote in 1742. But that's a whole different story, since by that time he'd given up on opera completely. Sometimes I feel like doing the same thing.

Teutonic
Tunesmiths

Haydn presented operas with strings attached

HAYDN

HAYDN ISN'T A NAME THAT LEAPS to mind when one thinks of composers of opera. Symphonies, yes – he wrote more than 100 of those. And about 52 piano sonatas and 84 string quartets, not to mention a dozen masses, four oratorios and about 160 chamber works for the baryton. (Writing for the baryton, an obscure instrument that resembles a cross between a cello and a guitar, became something of a specialty of Haydn's. His patron, Prince Nicholaus Esterhazy, was particularly fond of the instrument and would play it by the hour.) But it may surprise you to learn that Haydn wrote more than 20 operas. If titles such as *La fedelta premiata*, *La vera constanza*, *Il mondo della luna*, *Orlando Paladino* or *L'infedelta delusa* don't immediately ring a bell, don't worry. Hardly anyone else recognizes them, either.

Franz Joseph Haydn came from a humble background, born to a second-generation wheelwright in the tiny Austrian village of Rohrau, near the Hungarian border, in 1732. (Eighteenth-century political borders being less stable than they are today, it's possible, say some scholars, that when Haydn was born his village was under Hungarian rule. But calling him a Hungarian composer would only confuse matters unnecessarily, and they're confused enough already.)

As a boy, Haydn had a fine voice and sang in the choir of St. Stephen's Cathedral in Vienna. As Haydn approached puberty, the choirmaster, Georg Reutter, suggested that perhaps the boy should be castrated to preserve his lovely voice. But Haydn's father quickly nixed that idea. (Young Haydn's views on the subject have not been recorded, but it's probably safe to assume that he wasn't thrilled either. Would you be?)

Haydn wrote his first opera, *Der krumme Teufel* (The Crooked or Limping Devil) when he was just 19, and earning some extra money as a street musician in Vienna. He and his friends were serenading outside the house of the famous comic actor Johann Joseph Kurz, who performed under the name Kurz-Bernardon. The actor showed the young composer a short, comic libretto and that was that. Apparently, *Der krumme Teufel* was a great success and everybody thought it was hilariously funny. Everybody, that is, except a certain sourpuss nobleman, who thought the whole thing was intended to make fun of him, and had the work banned. Maybe it's only a coincidence that none of Haydn's music for this opera remains.

Haydn did the rest of his opera composing during his long association with the court of Prince Nicholaus Ester- hazy, who was always wanting him to write something. If it wasn't another baryton trio it was a new symphony, or an opera to celebrate the wedding of so-and-so or the name day of somebody else.

Prince Nicholaus was a bit of a showoff, really: he had a fabulous castle built way out in the country so he could spend his time hunting. (Duck-hunting in the streets of Vienna is frowned on by the local constabulary, even if you're a prince.) But the palace of Eszterhaza was not exactly a simple shack: in addition to its splendid sleeping chambers and fancy ballrooms, the palace had its own chapel, a separate hospital and not one but two theatres.

In the nearly 50 years that Haydn spent in the service of the Esterhazy family, he wrote 15 full operas for perform- ance in the prince's 400-seat opera house. Most of these are light, comic works, since 18th-century audiences liked to have a happy ending. (In Haydn's opera *Acide*, the death of the young shepherd hero Acis at the end would have displeased its audience, so the composer has him brought back to life by the sea-goddess Thetis. Acis returns in the form of a fountain and – as a fountain – joins in the closing quartet. You may think that's all wet, but Haydn's audiences lapped it up.)

Haydn's operas are rarely performed nowadays, having been overshadowed in popularity by the operas of that showoff, Mozart.

At least five of Haydn's other operas are neglected for another reason: he wrote them to be performed by marionettes. That was all very well for him: he had a patron with his very own marionette theatre. But how many of those have you seen lately? Marionette performers are getting harder to find: as actors, opera singers tend to be wooden, but not *that* wooden.

Besides, most entrepreneurs today would shy away from mounting a puppet performance. There are too many strings attached.

Masonic birds of a feather in The Magic Flute

MOZART

MOZART WROTE OPERAS AS EASILY AS the rest of
us write grocery lists – only his sound better and
they're a whole lot easier to listen to.

Mozart did try his hand at writing *opera seria* – including *Idomeneo* and *Lucio Silla* and another with a libretto by
Metastasio – but nobody remembers such heavyweight,
pompous works nowadays. We'd rather listen to his funny
ones.[1]

Wolfgang Amadeus Mozart was born in Salzburg on
January 27th, 1756 and showed such early ability for
music that his father, Leopold Mozart, a violinist and a bit
of a composer himself, almost immediately packed the boy
off on tour as a child prodigy. In the beginning he travelled
with his older sister, Anna Maria, whose nickname was
"Nannerl." She was clever but she wasn't half the whiz her
brother was. But then, neither was anyone else.

Leopold probably meant well, but there's no doubt he
gave the young Mozart a warped childhood. He was always
nagging his son about money and working hard and being
seen with the right people. Mozart couldn't help it. He just
wanted to have a good time.[2]

---

[1] Count Firmian paid Mozart 130 *gigliati* for composing *Lucio Scilla*. This
would mean more if we knew how much a *gigliati* would be worth today. Not
much, probably.

[2] Leopold Mozart wasn't a complete party-pooper. He once wrote a Hunting
Symphony that has a chorus for dogs and rifles.

Mozart wrote his first real opera, *La finta semplice*, in 1768. He was only 12 years old, but since he only lived to be 36 this was already one-third of the way through his career. (If he'd known, he probably would have started sooner.)

Other operas soon followed. After all, he had to have something to fill the time when he wasn't composing all those piano concertos, string quartets, masses, symphonies and more assorted chamber music than I can remember right now. Mozart liked to keep busy.[3]

Mozart's first operatic success came in 1782 with *Die Entfürung aus dem Serail*, or The Abduction From The Seraglio.[4] This is one of the first important operas written in German (as opposed to Italian) but the story follows a long tradition of so-called "rescue operas."[5]

The story is set in Turkey, in the harem of the Pasha Selim, where the hero Belmonte and his servant Pedrillo have come to rescue the hero's lover Constanze and her maid Blondchen (or "Blondie"). You might say they want to get the women out of harem's way.

They do this by getting the palace guard, a big fellow named Osmin, hopelessly drunk. They make their escape only to be recaptured, but the pasha eventually forgives them and everybody lives happily ever after – except for Osmin, who has a whopper of a hangover.

Mozart's score includes all sorts of twiddly bits on triangle, cymbal and drums that are supposed to sound like Turkish music. (He figured his Viennese audiences wouldn't know any better.)[6]

It may be only a coincidence, but it was just after the opening of *Die Entführung* that Mozart abducted his own

---

[3] In his spare moments he liked to gamble at cards and billiards. He usually lost.

[4] *Seraglio* is the Italian word for harem. There aren't as many of them now as there used to be.

[5] Following another long-established tradition in music, that of plagiarism, Mozart's librettist had shamelessly stolen the story from someone else.

[6] After hearing this opera, the Emperor Joseph II told Mozart that it was very nice but it had "far too many notes."

Constanze. Much against the wishes of his father, he married Constanze Weber, a cousin of the composer Carl Maria von Weber. She was the daughter of his landlady whose older sister Aloysia had earlier jilted him. Constance was flighty and irresponsible and not particularly attractive – in fact, a lot like Mozart himself. But he loved her anyway.[7]

Some of Mozart's best operas came when he teamed up with the librettist Lorenzo da Ponte, who's a story in himself. Da Ponte was born into a Jewish family in 1749 in Ceneda, Italy, as Emmanuel Conegliano. He later became Catholic and took an Italian name. In fact, he went so far as to become a priest, although this didn't seem to stop him from his favorite pursuits, which were gambling and chasing women. (Often in combination. Chasing women can be a gamble in itself.)

Pursued by creditors and enraged husbands, he eventually ended up in Vienna as a court poet for Joseph II. That's how he met Mozart, who by this time had landed a nearly steady job – steady for Mozart, anyway – composing for the emperor and for whoever else would pay him. (Finances were not Mozart's strong suit.) Between 1786 and 1790, da Ponte collaborated on three of Mozart's greatest comic operas: *Le Nozze di Figaro*, *Don Giovanni*, and *Cosi fan tutte*.[8]

Mozart's *Le nozze di Figaro* (The Marriage of Figaro) is a sequel to *Il barbiere di Siviglia* (The Barber of Seville), both based on two famous plays written by Pierre Augustin Caron de Beaumarchais. This confuses people who know only Rossini's version of *The Barber*, since Mozart wrote *Figaro* in 1786 but Rossini didn't write his *Barber* until 1816. This seems like the wrong order, but in Mozart's day everybody knew the *Barber* story from the opera written by

[7] He sometimes called her "Little Mouse."

[8] Da Ponte eventually moved to New York, where he became the first Italian teacher at Columbia University. He wrote an autobiography in which he hardly mentions Mozart at all, which is rather ungrateful of him, really.

Giovanni Paisiello in 1782. OK, got that?

Il barbiere di Siviglia (either version, take your pick) tells how Figaro, the barber, helps his master, Count Almavivo, win the hand of his lover Rosina against the intrigues of the physician Bartolo and the music teacher Don Basilio. *Le nozze di Figaro* has the same characters, plus a few (including a dotty old gardener named Antonio). It opens on Figaro's own wedding day to Susanna, the chambermaid of the new countess. (Figaro by this time has got himself promoted to be the count's valet.)

The opera's breezy overture lasts about four minutes – just about the right length for boiling an egg or steeping tea – after which follows a convoluted comic plot chock-full of disguises, intrigues, double-dealing and true love in which the servants finally come out on top.[9]

One of this opera's best-known soprano arias, "Voi che sapete" in Act II, is sung not by the *prima donna* role of Susanna but by her servant Cherubino, a soprano singing the role of a young man. Such a part, known as a "pants role," would as recently as 50 years before have been sung by a castrato. By this time, in more civilized Vienna, it was given to a woman. To make matters even more confusing, Cherubino sings the aria while disguised in Susanna's clothing, meaning she's a woman pretending to be a man disguised as a woman. This is why some people find opera so hard to follow.[10]

The second of the da Ponte librettos led to the opera that many consider to be Mozart's finest, *Don Giovanni*, a kind of morality play in which a notorious womanizer gets his comeuppance. Certainly it's one of his most entertaining and most popular. People like seeing a smooth operator at work, especially when they can feel self-righteously

[9] King Louis XVI of France had banned the original version of the play as being far too controversial, and Joseph II followed suit in Austria. There's nothing more dangerous, as Louis was to find out a few years later in 1789, than the common folk getting uppity.

[10] Just to round off the story, a German composer named Giselher Klebe wrote an opera in 1963 called *Figaro lässt sich scheiden*, or Figaro Gets Divorced.

smug when he gets punished at the end.

Da Ponte himself is said to have suggested using the well-known story of the amorous villain Don Juan, who in Italian becomes Don Giovanni. Da Ponte probably chose it because he knew where he could get hold of a libretto without much trouble. Most of the story is heavily "borrowed" from a Spanish version by Tirso de Molina and an Italian one by Carlo Goldoni. (Just to show that all's fair in love and libretto writing, Alexander Pushkin later stole the same story for an opera by the Russian composer Alexander Dargomizhsky called *The Stone Guest*.)

The title character in *Don Giovanni* should not be confused with any of the dozens of other Dons in Italian opera, such as Don Alfonzo in Donizetti's *Lucrezia Borgia*, or Don Alvaro and Don Carlo in Verdi's *La forza del destino*, or Don José in Bizet's *Carmen* (nor indeed with "La donna e mobile" from Verdi's *Rigoletto*, which is something else again). You'd think the Italians could pick another name now and then.

The opera opens with a quarrel between Don Giovanni and Donna Anna, a virtuous woman whom he has tried (and failed) to seduce. Her father, Don Pedro (a famous big shot known as *El Commendatore*) enters, fights with Don Giovanni and is killed. (It's a short part.) At this point, Don Giovanni shows his true colors by running away.

Donna Anna's fiancé, Don Ottavio – I told you there were too many Dons in this show – vows to avenge her father's death and that sets up the rest of the story.

Much of the comic relief in the opera comes from Don Giovanni's servant, Leporello, whose chief job in Act I is to sing the famous "Catalogue Aria" enumerating his master's many seductions. Just for the record, Leporello's list includes 640 in Italy, 231 in Germany, an even 100 in France, a mere 91 in Turkey and an astounding 1,003 in Spain (which after all is Don Giovanni's home turf, where presumably he has an advantage), all for a grand total of 2,065. Considering the number of successful conquests Don Giovanni manages in his own opera (i.e. zilch), we should be inclined to take Leporello's bragging with a large grain of salt. Another famous tune comes in the next scene, where Don Giovanni tries to seduce Zerlina with "La ci darem la mano." He strikes out there, too.[11]

Further deceptions, attempted seductions and narrow escapes follow, culminating with a scene in a graveyard, where Don Giovanni mockingly invites the statue of the dead Commendatore to dinner. This sets up the opera's climatic closing scene, in which the statue arrives on stage to drag the unrepentant Don Giovanni off to the fires of Hell. Hard luck. The opera ends with the survivors virtuously singing a chorus about true love and fidelity. This makes everybody feel better.[12]

Mozart managed to squeeze out two more operas, *Cosi fan tutte* and *La clemenza di Tito*, before starting work on what turned out to be his last opera and one of his final compositions.

Die Zauberflöte (The Magic Flute) is an odd little opera, a mystical tale full of strange symbolism and with a wildly unbelievable plot (not that *Don Giovanni* was exactly normal, mind you). It has a marvelous overture and such great tunes as The Queen of the Night's aria and the silly love duet between Papageno and Papagena, a couple of bird-brains.

Mozart wrote the opera for his friend Emanuel Schikaneder, a comic actor who wrote the libretto for a performance at a popular Viennese theatre.

This was not exactly a highbrow venue, but Mozart didn't mind at all: Schikaneder was paying him and the people seemed to like his work, and that was all that mattered to him. (Money was especially tight for Mozart at this point. He'd even dashed off some little pieces for

---

[11] Physically, Mozart was the very opposite of the suave and dashingly handsome Don Giovanni. The composer was short (about five foot four), with a head too big for his body, a pock-marked face from childhood chicken pox, squinty eyes (he was nearsighted) and a big nose.

[12] For reasons that escape me, a German translation of the opera for a performance in Mannheim in 1789 changes Don Giovanni's name to Herr von Schwänkerich. Leporello becomes, of all things, Fickfack.

mechanical clock because he needed the cash.)

Scholars nowadays like to make a game of finding all sorts of important symbolism in *The Magic Flute*, including allusions to secret Masonic rituals. There's even a theory that Mozart's sudden death in 1791 at the age of 36 was part of a plot by Masons disgruntled that he had given away their trade secrets.[13]

Another theory, first dramatized in the Rimsky-Korsakov opera *Mozart And Salieri* and most recently revived by the popular play and movie Amadeus, was that Mozart was poisoned by his jealous rival, the court composer Antonio Salieri.

You can believe all of that if you want to. It certainly makes a great bedtime story. But if you ask me, the answer to Mozart's sudden death is much more simple: it was writing all those operas that finally did him in.

---

[13] Masons are touchy about such things. God knows why.

Four walls do not a Fidelio make

BEETHOVEN

S INCE HE WROTE ONLY ONE OPERA, Beethoven's contribution to the history of the genre might hardly be worth considering. But he is, after all, Beethoven.

Ludwig van Beethoven was born in Bonn on December 16th, 1770 and spent his early years as a performing prodigy. (In this he was rather shamelessly encouraged by his father, who was a better drunk than he was a musician.) By 1792, Beethoven had moved to Vienna, the cultural centre of Europe, where he intended to make a name for himself as a concert pianist and composer.

Proper Viennese society didn't quite know what to make of Beethoven: he was arrogant, impolite, disrespectful and, well, downright rude. But he could play the piano and write music like nobody's business, so they tended to forgive him.

It was in Vienna that Beethoven came to appreciate the operas of other composers of the day. (He found it so much easier to listen to an opera than to write one. It took so much less time. I'm the same way myself.)

Beethoven saw most of his opera performances at Vienna's Theatre an der Wien. This was especially convenient because that's where Beethoven was living at the time, in a little apartment in the theatre building itself. All he had to do was cross the hall. He liked to take a seat in the front row near the orchestra pit, where he would sit immobile as a statue through the whole performance. Unless, of course, he decided he didn't like it, in which case he'd sneak out at the end of the first act.

"He was," writes Beethoven's friend Ignaz von Seyfried, a fellow musician, "particularly captivated by the works of Cherubini and Mehul." That would be Etienne Nicolas Mehul, a French composer of some 30 operas, quite famous in his day and much admired by Napoleon. Unfortunately for Mehul, when Napoleon's influence declined, so did the composer's. That's politics for you.

Beethoven himself completed only one opera, but not for lack of trying. Emanuel Schikaneder, who wrote the libretto for Mozart's The Magic Flute, tried to interest Beethoven in his libretto Vesta's Fire, but nothing much ever came of it. Other opera projects that Beethoven toyed with briefly before discarding – in his bad moods he had a short attention span – included librettos about Brutus, Romulus and The Homecoming Of Ulysses.

But finally Beethoven found a subject that interested him. The story tells how Florestan, being held prisoner for his political beliefs by the corrupt official Pizarro, is rescued by his loving wife, Leonore. She does this by disguising herself as a man and calling herself Fidelio. (There's a lot more to it than that, so don't try this at home unless you know the whole story.) Opera historian Henry Edward Krehbiel points out, rather approvingly, I think, that Fidelio is one of the few operas "which hymns the pure love of married lovers." He's got a point, you know, especially when you consider the adultery in Mozart's operas, not to mention the incest in Wagner's.

One of the highlights of Fidelio comes at the end of the first act, when all the prisoners are briefly released from the darkness of their prison cells. Their chorus in praise of freedom, "O welche Lust!" (which is actually about light, and not about what you might think) is always a poignant moment. (Maybe it goes over so well because audience members can relate to the feeling: they know the intermission is coming up any minute.)

Since Beethoven's opera is all about Leonore and Florestan, it is naturally called Fidelio. Beethoven never liked the title – he thought it spoiled the surprise – and he himself titled it Leonore for its first performance, in 1805.

The first performance, sad to tell, was a bit of a

disaster. Napoleon had chosen just that time to invade Vienna, so all the opera-loving nobility had bravely scurried out of town. Hardly anyone showed up for the premiere of Beethoven's new work. (Performing an opera about political freedom in the middle of a military occupation was probably not the most sensible thing to be doing at that point. It's a good thing that Napoleon's French troops couldn't understand German.)

The performance went badly for other reasons, too. The role of Leonore was sung by soprano Pauline Anna Milder-Hauptmann – a singer whom Haydn had once said had "a voice as big as a house" – and she complained to the composer that the notes were too difficult. Of the other roles, stage director Georg Friedrich Treitschke tells us that "the men left all the more to be desired." One member of the audience, the diarist Joseph Carl Rosenbaum, wrote that "the opera contains pretty, artistic and difficult music, a boring, not very interesting book. It was not a success, and the theatre was empty." In fact, he concludes, "the whole is distinguishable neither by invention nor execution." Everybody's a critic.

After the opening-night disaster, Beethoven's friends convinced him to do a little trimming and rewriting, which helped a little but not enough. He even composed a new overture, something he'd also tried before. But it didn't help that time, either.

Finally, in 1814, after letting it rest for nine years, Beethoven revised *Fidelio* a third time, and the opera was greeted with greater enthusiasm (not the least because it was considerably shorter). By now, his one opera had four different overtures. The first three are now referred to as the Leonore Overtures (numbers 1, 2 and 3) and the fourth one is the Fidelio Overture. Some scholars argue that we've been getting the numbers wrong all these years, and that the piece we call the Leonore Overture No. 2 should really be the Leonore Overture No. 1. I say let them argue. Incidentally, Beethoven's final Fidelio Overture wasn't quite ready for the opening night of the revised performance, so the orchestra played The Ruins Of Athens instead. Well, they had to play *something*.

Russian
Into Things

*Mussorgsky and Rimsky-Korsakov
reflect on Boris Godunov*

GLINKA / THE MIGHTY FIVE / TCHAIKOVSKY

OPERA IN RUSSIA GOT OFF to a slow start, mostly because music in Russia got off to a slow start, too. The kind of music, at least, that leads to opera – formal, book-learned music with key signatures and tempo markings and reams and reams of little black dots all over the paper.

Ordinary Russians had been singing folk songs and whooping it up for hundreds and hundreds of years, but nobody had bothered to write much of it down.[1]

Peter the Great, who began his reign in the late 17th century, didn't care much for opera, which was still just getting started anyway. As a boy he sang briefly in the court choir, but when he grew up he was more the military band type. Peter wasn't called "the Great" for nothing: he grew up to be nearly seven feet tall. He was so strong he could take a silver serving platter and twist it into a scroll.[2]

Peter's daughter, Elizabeth, liked opera enough to have a theatre built, but she had a hard time convincing the nobles to go to the performances. She had to go door to door and ask. (Sometimes she had to remind the really reluctant ones that they should do it as a favor to her – and after all,

---

[1] A lot of Russian folk music also includes dancing, and some of it involves whirling around the room throwing knives into the floor. This can be quite exciting to watch, as long as you keep your toes out of the way.

[2] This is the kind of showy party trick that may be impressive the first time you see it, but loses its appeal after a while—especially if it's your platter he's using.

71

she *was* the empress.)

It was during the reign of another Great – Catherine the Great – that opera became more of a regular occurrence in Russia. (How Catherine came to be empress of all Russia is an interesting story, but a complicated one. First of all, her name wasn't Catherine: it was Princess Sophia Augusta Frederica of Anhalt-Zerbst. Besides that, she wasn't even really Russian: she was German.)

Catherine loved opera, especially comic French opera (she didn't really have the attention span for anything very serious). She invited such famous composers as Salieri and Paisiello to visit St. Petersburg and perform operas of their own and by others. In the last quarter of the 18th century, historian Donald Jay Grout tells us, nearly 350 operas had their premiere performances in Russia.[3]

But even those operas weren't really *Russian* ones, since they weren't written by Russian composers and they weren't sung in Russian. It took a composer named Mikhail Ivanovich Glinka (1804-57) to establish a truly national style of opera. (He did this at the same time he was establishing a truly national style of composing everything else, too, so that made it a whole lot easier.)

Glinka came from a wealthy family and a long line of layabouts. He was raised by his invalid grandmother, who wrapped him in furs so he wouldn't catch a cold. As a boy, Glinka liked nothing better than the sound of banging copper pots together. He eventually outgrew this, but not before severely damaging most of Granny's best kitchen-ware. Sometimes his father would hire a small orchestra to play music at dinner, and little Mikhail especially liked hearing the band play the old Russian folk songs. (Pay attention, now: this becomes important later on.)

Glinka is known for two operas, *A Life For The Tsar* and *Russlan And Ludmilla*.[4] Neither of them was a roaring

---

[3] I'm prepared to believe him: I've found it's not a good idea to disagree with Grout.

[4] Some people like spell *Russlan* with only one s and *Ludmilla* with only one l after the first one. I don't have a preference myself.

success at the time, but now we can see just how important they were. Glinka wrote the overture for *A Life For The Tsar* before writing the rest of the opera. This is generally considered bad form. The first performance of *Russlan*, in 1842, was so bad that even some of the singers and orchestra members booed the production. This is also generally considered bad form.[5] Neither of Glinka's operas is performed much nowadays, even in Russia, although the overture to *Russlan* shows up now and then in the concert hall or on highbrow radio stations. It's got some good tunes and it fills out the program nicely.

But what's significant about Glinka's operas is that he used a lot of old Russian folk songs as the melodies. (See, I told you this was important.) Not only did this save him a lot of time, it also made it much easier for audiences to leave the theatre whistling the tunes. It nearly guarantees success.

The group of composers who followed Glinka knew a good thing when they saw it, and so nearly all of their music contains bits of Russian folk songs to give it that special ethnic flavor.

These five composers – Mily Balakirev, César Cui, Alexander Borodin, Nicolai Rimsky-Korsakov and Modest Mussorgsky – established the first wave of Russian nationalism in music and came to be known as The Mighty Five or The Mighty Handful. (In Russian it's *Moguchaya Kuchka*, or "The Mighty Little Heap." I won't say a heap of what.)

None of them was a full-time composer: they nearly all had cushy government jobs. Cui was a journalist who became a general in the Russian army. He spent most of his time teaching soldiers how to dig trenches and how to sneak up on the enemy. Mussorgsky lost his inheritance in a government purge and ended up working as a clerk in the ministry of forests. Borodin taught chemistry at the state academy.

[5] Constantine Bachturin was drunk when he wrote the plot outline, which may have had something to do with it.

Balakirev wrote no operas and Borodin wrote only one that anyone remembers, *Prince Igor* (and even then they can only hum you bits from the Polovtsian Dances). Rimsky-Korsakov wrote 14, of which the only one I can recall is *Mozart And Salieri* (1898). This is the one that says Salieri poisoned Mozart because he was jealous. Well, who wouldn't be?

Cui wrote 10 operas, but no less an authority than Grout himself tells us that "with the possible exception of *William Ratcliffe* (1869), they are unimportant from any point of view." There you have it.[6] It fell to Mussorgsky to compose the one Russian opera of any consequence, his great tragedy *Boris Godunov*.

Mussorgsky was one of those difficult artistic types, a man of great creative genius but slovenly habits. When he wasn't being brilliant, he was an arrogant, temperamental brooder who drank far more than was good for him. (Despite his name, Modest Mussorgsky was anything but modest: in his memoirs he refers to himself entirely in the third person.)

He had trouble keeping a job and he was almost always short of cash. One summer night in 1875, coming home to find that his landlord had locked him out, Mussorgsky wandered the streets of St. Petersburg until early in the morning, when he found himself at the door of his friend Naumof. Being the generous sort, Naumof invited him in to sleep the rest of the night on the couch. Mussorgsky stayed for the next three years.

But despite his personal problems, Mussorgsky found the time to compose such masterpieces as Pictures At An Exhibition (which he wrote for piano but which sounds much more impressive in the version Rimsky-Korsakov did for orchestra) and the opera *Boris Godunov*. He took a stab at writing four other operas, but he didn't manage to finish any of them. He had trouble concentrating.

[6] In his journalism, Cui was a big supporter of the Russian nationalism of his buddies, but even he had his standards. *Ratcliffe* had seven good performances in 1869, but the eighth was so bad that even Cui panned it in the paper the next day.

Even *Boris* gave him trouble: he finished the first version in 1869 but rewrote it in 1872. A complete version was finally performed in 1874. Rimsky-Korsakov took a crack at revising it in 1896 and again in 1908. If he heard it today, Mussorgsky might have trouble recognizing parts of it.

Based, like nearly all Russian operas, on a story by Pushkin, Mussorgsky's opera tells how Boris Godunov, a onetime friend of Czar Ivan the Terrible, becomes czar by secretly murdering Ivan's infant son, Dmitri. Boris later has the throne taken from him by a young monk named Grigori, who claims that he is actually the grown Dmitri miraculously brought back to life. In the dramatic closing scene, racked with guilt and remorse, Boris prays God for mercy and sings his big dying scene.

Mussorgsky's opera is one of the few that gives its juiciest role not to a soprano or a tenor, but to a bass. In my opinion, this should be done far more often. Most operatic tenors, like small children, should be seen but not heard.[7]

The most famous Boris of all was the Russian bass Feodor Chaliapin, who was known not only for his booming voice but also for his ability to act convincingly – a rare, not to say almost unique, achievement for an operatic singer. He was a great singer and a great actor – and he wasn't afraid to admit it to anybody. (He was also a great drinker, which he'd admit pretty readily as well.)

Chaliapin was a big man in every sense of the word: he stood six foot six inches tall in his stocking feet (he'd have made a good Peter the Great) and he when he wasn't on stage he liked to wear a raccoon coat with a big checked hat. He commanded enormous fees for his performances, arguing that he needed the money to feed his 12 children. (He had eight by his first wife, four by his second.) One of Chaliapin's greatest successes came in his performance as Boris at the Metropolitan Opera in New York in 1921.

---

[7] The cast of *Boris Godunov* includes one character called "An Idiot." The role is of course sung by a tenor.

Chaliapin sang his part in Russian and everyone else sang theirs in Italian. No one seemed to mind at all.

In a completely different camp from The Mighty Five was the composer Tchaikovsky. In fact, they had as little to do with each other as possible. The Five thought Tchaikovsky's music wasn't nearly Russian enough (what it needed, they said, was more folk songs), while Tchaikovsky thought they were all a bunch of giftless amateurs who wouldn't know a good melody if it came up and bit one of them on the leg.[8]

Nowadays nobody much thinks of Tchaikovsky as an opera composer, even though he wrote at least eight of them (not including a few that he never finished). This is hardly surprising, since even Tchaikovsky himself thought his operas weren't really very important in the grand scheme of things.[9]

Tchaikovsky might have written more operas – or more operas you'd have heard of, at least – if his personal life hadn't been so, well, complicated. It seems there was always something getting in the way.

Peter Ilyich Tchaikovsky was born in May, 1840 in the Russian town of Kamsko-Votkinsk.[10] His mother was a cultured woman who spoke fluent French and enjoyed music. His father was a mining engineer who thought his son should study law and get a good job.

Little Peter was a sensitive child who showed an early appreciation for music (though not when the tunes he heard in his head kept him awake all night, which made him cranky). His first exposure to opera came from hearing tunes from Mozart's *Don Giovanni* on a little music box owned by his parents. This established his lifelong appre-

[8] Rimsky-Korsakov eventually said a few nice things about some of Tchaikovsky's music, but it was too late to make amends.

[9] He's right, too. They aren't.

[10] If you want to sound more Russian, you can spell has first name Piotr. But I refuse to go along with the current trend toward spelling his surname Chaikovsky or Chaikovski. Some deranged librarian thought this up just to torment us.

ciation of Mozart's music.[11] As a young man, he had quite a fine voice and could perform arias from the operas of Rossini, Bellini and Donizetti. He did this at parties sometimes, to impress his friends.

Like the members of The Mighty Five, Tchaikovsky got his first job with the government, in the department of justice. This pleased his father, even though Tchaikovsky was just a lowly law clerk. But soon he quit the job to study music at the St. Petersburg Academy, which was led by the famous pianist and composer Anton Rubenstein.[12]

When he wasn't writing piano music or symphonies or ballet scores or the 1812 Overture, Tchaikovsky tried his hand at writing opera. It seemed like the thing to do.

He wrote a couple of operas named *Voevoda* and *Undine* but most of that music has since gotten lost somewhere, which is probably just as well. (He did steal a march from *Undine* and use it again in his Symphony No. 2, just so it wouldn't go to waste.)

He started work on an opera named *Mandragora* but later abandoned it because his friends told him the story was just too silly. The only surviving piece from this is a chorus sung by a bunch of insects, which probably gives you the general idea.

Around 1874 he wrote another opera, called *The Oprichnik*, which is all about the secret police of Ivan the Terrible. It wasn't very popular at the time and is even less so now, secret police still being something of a touchy subject in Soviet Russia, even after *glasnost*.[13]

Also in 1874, Tchaikovsky wrote another opera, which

---

[11] On the other hand, Tchaikovsky had a lifelong hatred of the music of Wagner. Maybe this would have been different if he'd heard "The Ride of the Valkyries" on a music box. Maybe, but I doubt it.

[12] Rubenstein never liked Tchaikovsky's music very much. He especially disliked the young composer's B-flat piano concerto, which he called "unplayable." He eventually learned to play it anyway, when he saw that everyone else was doing it.

[13] The official government censor had given Tchaikovsky a rough time over *The Oprichnik*. He thought the story made Czar Ivan look just a bit too terrible.

he called *Vakula The Smith*. He composed it hoping to win the prize in an opera-writing competition put on by the Russian Musical Society. But in his haste he misjudged the deadline and got it finished a whole year ahead of schedule, which the other entrants thought was very unsporting of him. (It made them look bad.) For a performance in 1876 he changed the title to *Tcherevichky* or *The Shoes*. That didn't make it any more popular.[14]

The one opera that Tchaikovsky always wanted to write but never did was one based on Shakespeare's story of Romeo and Juliet. The composer did manage to write a ballet score (which became a big hit when he worked it into a concert overture) but he never did write the opera. Too bad. It might have been fun. Vladimir Stassov, a busybody who was an important friend of The Mighty Five, once wrote a letter to Tchaikovsky, telling him he'd made a big mistake leaving out the nurse in his Romeo and Juliet ballet.[15]

Tchaikovsky's personal life during all this time was, to put it mildly, rather confused. It's a wonder he got anything written at all.

It was while working on *Voevoda* that Tchaikovsky met a French soprano named Desiree Artot, with whom he thought he fell in love. He was all ready to propose marriage to her but she up and married someone else. (He was the Spanish baritone Mariano Padillay Ramos, who never amounted to much.) Historians will tell you that Desiree Artot is the only woman Tchaikovsky ever loved. After her, he didn't try very hard.

He actually did get married for a while there, in 1877 to a woman named Antonia Miliukova. She threw herself at him, and he didn't know what else to do.[16] But their marriage was a fiasco that lasted all of about nine weeks. They just weren't right for each other: Antonia was a little lacking in the intellectual department, and Tchaikovsky had some problems of his own.

[14] Nor did changing the name again to *The Caprices Of Oxana*. It was still the same opera.

[15] Tchaikovsky made up for it by putting a nurse in his opera *Eugene Onegin*.

[16] After they got married he was really out of his depth.

The marriage upset him so much that Tchaikovsky even attempted suicide by wading into the River Neva, hoping he might drown or at least catch pneumonia or something. All he got was wet.

On the operatic front, strangely enough, Tchaikovsky was steaming full ahead. Just before the marriage he had begun work on what became his only successful opera, *Eugene Onegin*, the story of a gallivanting man and his romances that comes across as a kind of watered-down *Don Giovanni*. (There's that Mozart influence for you.)

He wrote a few more operas, including *The Queen Of Spades*, which displayed the composer's knowledge of cards.[17] He also wrote a version of *Iolanthe* 10 years before Gilbert and Sullivan got hold of the story. Tchaikovsky's *Iolanthe* had its premiere in 1892, the same time as the premiere of his ballet music for *The Nutcracker* – a work that everybody loves except Tchaikovsky himself. (He thought it was "infinitely worse than *Sleeping Beauty*.")

I now realize we've come nearly to the end of Tchaikovsky's life and I haven't yet mentioned anything about Nadejda von Meck. What's there to say? She was a wealthy widow with 11 children and pots of money. Around about 1876, when she was 46 and Tchaikovsky 10 years younger, she wrote him a fan letter and offered him as much money as he needed to keep composing. They never met face to face (though they did accidentally bump into each other on the road one time) and for most of his life they wrote letters back and forth. She sent him money and he dedicated music to her. It seemed like a pretty good arrangement – for him, at least.

If you ask me, Tchaikovsky would have been better to forget about writing operas entirely and concentrate on symphonies or ballets. He was so much better at them. Can you imagine a ballet version of *The Oprichnik*, with secret police in tutus doing pirouette's all over the place? Now *that* would be something.

---

[17] He was especially fond of whist. His friend Nikolai Rubenstein (Anton's kid brother) was a terrible gambler.

Ulterior
Leitmotifs

Richard slays another dragon

WAGNER

IT'S DIFFICULT TO KNOW WHICH IS more detestable, Wagner's music or Wagner himself. What do you say about a man who was arrogant, mean-spirited, racist and aggressively self-centred? What do you say about operas that are tedious, time-consuming and loud enough to cause hearing loss?

Well, you can say either that Wagner was a musical mastermind or that he wasn't, that his operas are the pinnacle of creative achievement or that they're over-rated rot, that Wagner himself was an intellectual genius or an obnoxious boor. Which of those alternatives you choose might depend significantly on who else is in the room when you do it.

The musical world can pretty much be divided into two camps: those who think Wagner's works represent the highest achievement of the operatic ideal, and those who can't understand what all the shouting is about.

I belong to the second group and I don't care who knows it. "Wagner is a man devoid of all talent," César Cui wrote to Rimsky-Korsakov in 1863. A review in the Parisian magazine Figaro in 1876 called Wagner's operas "the music of a demented eunuch." This is surely unfair to eunuchs, and if there are any of them left out there, they might consider launching a class-action libel suit.

I wouldn't go quite that far – after all, he did write some great tunes – but there's no doubt that, like a talkative bore, Wagner's music tends to overstay its welcome.

"Wagner has good moments," said Rossini, "but bad quarter-hours." That just about says it all. When Rossini said, "How wonderful opera would be if there were no singers!" he must have been thinking of Wagner.[1]

Wilhelm Richard Wagner (he later dropped the Wilhelm) was born in Leipzig in 1813. His mother, the former Johanna Pätz, was a baker's daughter. Her husband at the time was a police official named Friedrich Wagner, who died shortly after the boy was born.

A little while later, Johanna married Ludwig Geyer, a painter, actor and poet who had been hanging around the Wagner house for quite some time. Friends used to remark on how much Johanna's boy resembled Geyer, whereas the boy hardly looked like the older Wagner at all. Maybe it was just a coincidence.

As a boy, Richard used the surname Geyer until his early teens, until he changed it back to Wagner. Maybe he realized that people would find it just too difficult to speak of "Geyerian" opera. "Wagnerian" has a much better ring to it, you must agree.

As a child, Wagner was what you might call a handful.[2] Sometimes, for no apparent reason, he would let out a scream loud enough to peel the paint. The characters in his operas tend to do this, too.

In school he spent less time going to classes than he did writing a long and convoluted play called *Leubald*, which he fancied as a sort of Shakespearean tragedy.

Like Shakespeare's Hamlet, Wagner's hero is confronted by the ghost of his murdered father. Unlike Hamlet, Leubald takes more direct action as vengeance: he kills just about everybody he can get his hands on and ends up going mad. By the end of the fourth act, so many characters are dead that Wagner had to bring some of them back in the fifth as ghosts so the plot would work out.

---

[1] "After *Lohengrin*, I had a splitting headache," wrote Mily Balakirev to Vladimir Stasov in 1868, "and all through the night I dreamed about a goose."

[2] His boyhood nickname was "Cossack."

Wagner took sporadic music lessons from a man named Müller, but there's no sense blaming Müller: as a composer, Wagner was largely self-taught. This probably explains a lot. He developed a great admiration for the music of Beethoven, especially the Ninth Symphony, which he studied by copying out the complete score by hand.[3]

Wagner wrote his first complete opera, a variation on the old Orpheus legend called *Die Feen* (The Fairies), in 1834, though he never saw it performed in his lifetime. He tried to convince the directors of the Leipzig opera house to produce it but they wouldn't bite.

Later that year, Wagner landed a job directing a small opera company in Magdeburg, even though his qualifications for the position were less than impressive: he was a clumsy pianist and a mediocre singer at best and he had minimal conducting experience, but they hired him anyway.[4]

It was there that he met and soon married one of the singers, Christiane Wilhelmine Planer, known as Minna. It was a package deal: she was nearly four years older than he was and already had a nine-year-old daughter named Natalie, whom she tried to pass off as her sister.

Wagner and Minna were married for 25 years, and they were happy together for the first few of them, anyway. At the start, Minna was pretty and affectionate and Wagner was passionate and boyishly charming. (On their first date he became so drunk he spent the night passed out on her couch.) But later on the marriage fell apart. Between his moodiness and numerous affairs, and her depression and constant nagging, somehow all the fun went out of the relationship. Wagner fell back on the old complaint that his wife didn't understand him. Who could?

But that was later on. In the beginning they were a

---

[3] Maybe the problem with modern music is that nobody does this kind of thing anymore.

[4] He came highly recommended by the Leipzig people, who saw it as an easy way of getting rid of both the composer and his opera.

team: he wrote operas and she told him how wonderful they were. It seemed to be working fine.[5]

Wagner got things rolling with a series of early operas, including *Das Liebesvorbot* (The Love Ban), based on Shakespeare's Measure For Measure, *Rienzi*, *Die fliegende Holländer* (The Flying Dutchman), *Tannhäuser* and *Lohengrin*, each of which grows louder than the one before. Wagner felt he was on to something.

It was around this time that Wagner met the pianist and composer Franz Liszt, who became one of his staunch admirers. When he could, Liszt would lend Wagner money when he needed it, which was most of the time. Wagner also met Liszt's daughter Cosima, who soon began admiring him in a more direct manner.

Cosima, whose nickname was "Stork," was married at the time to the conductor Hans von Bülow, who remained a champion of Wagner's music even after he discovered that the composer and his wife had grown, well, rather friendly. (Wagner and Cosima Liszt von Bülow had three children : Isolde, Eva and Siegfried. They even got married before the last one.)[6]

When he wasn't writing grandiose operas, Wagner liked to spout off on a variety of subjects, most of which he knew little or nothing about. This didn't stop him.

He wrote about the virtues of being German and the trouble with everybody who wasn't – especially the Jews. Adolf Hitler thought Wagner and his music were the greatest thing since sliced bread, which ought to give you the general idea.

Wagner thought everyone should become vegetarian. If we all stopped killing animals and ate only fruits and vegetables, he said, the world would be a better place.

---

[5] In Wagner's first drafts of *Die fliegende Holländer*, the faithful heroine's name is not Senta but Minna.

[6] Between Minna and Cosima, Wagner had spent an evening or several with Mathilde Wesendonk, Jessie Laussot, Julie Schwabe, Judith Gautier, a couple of teenaged daughters of a pork butcher in Prague, and Cosima's older sister, Blandine Ollivier. Maybe others, too.

Realizing this would be harder for people living in northern climates, he suggested helpfully that we should all move to the equator, where the growing season is longer. The lakes in the north of Canada, he wrote, are chock-full of vegetarian panthers and tigers.[7] Wagner, by the way, seems to have been a vegetarian more in theory than in practice. He liked to sneak some meat onto his plate now and then.

His biggest scheme came in his theories about art. Having decided, for reasons that remain unclear to me, that the best art should take its inspiration from pre-Christian mythology, Wagner set out to create an epic saga of music, drama, poetry and the visual arts that would combine everything into what he called *Gesamtkuntswerk*, which is German for "the whole ball of wax" – or words to that effect.

To do this, he developed the concept of the *leitmotif*, a kind of musical introduction bureau in which all the major characters, and many important objects, in an opera have their own little musical signature tune. This can be a useful trick, but not if you take it to extremes. Claude Debussy felt that the use of *leitmotifs* "suggests a world of harmless lunatics who present their visiting cards and shout their name in song."

Wagner also developed a style of writing that did away with the traditional format of recitatives and arias. Instead, he strung everything together into what he called *unendlich Melodie*, or "endless melody." It isn't actually endless, but it sure seems that way when you're listening to it.

Wagner put his theories to work (not to mention putting his listeners to work) in his enormous opera cycle *Der Ring des Nibelungen*, or The Ring of the Nibelung.[8]

The four operas of The Ring Cycle (just for the record, they are *Das Rheingold*, *Die Walküre*, *Siegfried* and *Götterdämmerung*) tell a convoluted story based on old

[7] This may have been true in Wagner's day. But there weren't any left last time I looked.

[8] Nibelung is difficult to translate: it means a kind of dwarf.

Norse mythology. Ready? Here goes:

Three young women, named Flosshilde, Wellgunde and Wogelinde, are living at the bottom of the Rhine River (it's a damp basement apartment, but the rent's cheap), where they are guarding over a bunch of gold. The misshapen dwarf Alberich renounces love and steals the gold, using it to make a magical ring to give him ultimate power.

Meanwhile, the head god Wotan has hired Fasolt and Fafner, a giant contracting firm, to build him Valhalla, a kind of retirement resort for dead heroes. Unable to pay them (a situation Wagner would know from firsthand experience), Wotan steals the ring and the gold from Alberich. Persuaded by his wife Fricka and the earth-goddess Erda, Wotan gives the giants the gold and the ring after they threaten to break his kneecaps, whereupon Fafner kills Fasolt and takes the whole lot for himself.

Through Erda, Wotan fathers nine daughters, called the Valkyries, to defend Valhalla. Then he goes to Earth and fathers two human children, the girl Sieglinde and the boy Siegmund. (Remember those names, they come back later in the story.) Sieglinde marries Hunding, who lives in a hut with a tree growing in the middle of it – which is all right if you want the rustic look. Siegmund, meanwhile, takes off to go backpacking around Europe. That introduces most of the important characters and gets us to the end of *Das Rheingold*. Whew!

Die Walküre opens in Hunding's hut, where Siegmund has wandered in, thinking it might be a youth hostel. He makes eyes at Sieglinde, not realizing she's his sister (he's been on the road awhile). They run off, having stolen the magical sword Nothung, carelessly left behind by Wotan.

Hunding, needless to say, is upset, though whether more about the sword than his wife is difficult to know. Backed by Wotan, the jealous Hunding kills Siegmund, destroying the sword in the process. But Brünnhilde, one of the Valkyries, sides with Siegmund against Daddy's wishes. She gives the broken sword to Sieglinde, so Wotan makes her stand in the corner on a burning rock until she agrees to behave. (Brünnhilde's fiery closing scene, and the ear-piercing aria that goes with it, tends to distract from the other eight Valkyries. Their names, in case anyone asks you, are Gerhilde, Grimgerde, Helmwige, Ortlinde, Rossweise, Schwertleite, Siegrune and Waltraute. Now you know.)

The third part of the cycle is *Siegfried*, named after its hero, the son of Sieglinde and Siegmund (who, by the way, are both his parents and his aunt and uncle), born some-time between the previous opera and this one.[9]

Siegfried is being raised by Mime, another dwarf, who happens to be the brother of Alberich. Mime (who despite his name does, in fact, sing) helps Siegfried restore the magic sword.[10] Mime seems like a nice guy, but secretly he's hoping to get the magic ring for himself. You can't trust anybody in these operas.

Learning of Mime's treachery (a little birdie told him so), Siegfried kills the dwarf after having killed the giant Fafner, who by this time had turned himself into a dragon to protect his investment. With his sword and the magic ring, Siegfried runs through the fire and rescues Brünhilde so they can live happily ever after.

That might have been a good place to end the story, but Wagner, being a pessimist, decided he had to be thorough. The final segment, *Götterdämmerung*, is even more confus-ing than all the others put together, if that's possible.

In this opera, everybody and his half-brother wants the ring but doesn't get it, while nobody who gets the ring really wants it. What can I say? In the end, everybody dies, Valhalla burns to a crisp, the Rhine overflows its banks, sweeping everything away, and we end up back at the bottom of the river – exactly where we started hours and hours and hours ago. The whole thing, you might say, is a washout.

That's it. That's The Ring – the opera cycle that gets its name, obviously, because by the end of the ordeal the

---

[9] The Ring has long intermissions, which makes this easier.

[10] "It was Nothung," he says.

weary listener wants to wring Wagner's neck.

None of Wagner's other operas, not *Die Meistersinger von Nürnberg* nor *Tristan und Isolde* nor *Parsifal*, can hold a candle to The Ring in either length, loudness or mind-numbing complexity.

The Ring made Wagner the rich, successful composer he'd always wanted to be, and in the years before his death in 1883 he liked nothing better than to lounge in the lap of luxury. He composed most of *Parsifal*, his last opera, after soaking for hours in a hot bath scented with perfume. He had his own full-time seamstress, whose name was Bertha Goldwag, to make him clothing made from expensive satin and silk and fur, and he liked pink silk underwear. Bertha made him 24 silk dressing gowns, many of them lined with fur. Well, whatever turns you on.

"All artists need stimulants of some kind," writes biographer Ernest Newman (somewhat defensively, I think), "and the touch of a fine fabric may have been necessary to send the thrill of inspiration through Wagner's nervous system – the thrill that other and less fortunate men have to get from women or from wine."

If wearing pink silk underwear or furry dressing gowns is what it takes to be an inspired artist, I'm just as happy to be one of those "less fortunate men" who has to rely on women or wine, thanks all the same.

Italian Sausage
Machines

The original sausage machine of Italian opera

VIVALDI

VIVALDI IS ONE OF THE MOST prolific composers in the history of music. There are a lot of other ways to describe him, but "prolific" is probably the most kind. He's living proof (well, dead proof now) of how much you can accomplish if you really apply yourself.

Reactions to Vivaldi's music have always been somewhat mixed. In his heyday he was highly regarded for both his playing and his compositions, but not everyone was so easily impressed. His contemporary Carlo Goldoni described him as "an excellent violin player and a mediocre composer." The 18th-century English diarist Charles Burney classed him "among the light and irregular troops." Still, you've got to admit, he was prolific.

Antonio Lucio Vivaldi was born in Venice in 1678 (or, depending on your source of information, 1675).[1] His father was a baker's son who became a professional violinist and his mother was a tailor's daughter. If nothing else, their children were well fed and clothed. Like his father, Vivaldi's most striking features were a rather large, hooked nose and his red hair, which earned him the nickname *il prete rossa*, or "the red priest." Other than that, notes one biographer, "the features of the face are vague and a little sheeplike."[2]

The young Vivaldi prepared himself for the priesthood

---

[1] Or 1669.
[2] His music's a little sheeplike too.

but although he was ordained in 1703 he hardly ever said Mass. Fanciful biographers have attributed this to his habit of zipping out of the sanctuary to jot down some new musical theme or other, but Vivaldi himself says that he suffered from a chest ailment that today we might call asthma. (Or maybe it had something to do with that irregularity Burney talked about.)

Yet despite his weak health, and the demands of a full-time job as violin teacher at a school for orphaned girls, Vivaldi found the time to write nearly 500 concertos, a whole bunch of church music and, at last count, nearly 50 operas – making him the first of the operatic Italian sausage machines. (Vivaldi himself says he wrote 94 operas, but he was known to exaggerate.) He also, by the way, found the time to become rather friendly with one of his singing pupils, a French wigmaker's daughter named Anna Giraud. (And also, some said, with her sister Paolina, though whether simultaneously or sequentially I'm not prepared to say.)

Vivaldi wrote his first opera, *Ottone in Villa*, in 1713, to a libretto by Domenico Lalli. Lalli's real name was Sebastino Biancardi, but he'd changed it when he had to leave Naples in a hurry. (There was that small matter of the embezzlement charge.)

Other Vivaldi operas soon followed, in rapid succession, including such works as *Orlando finto pazzo*, *Argippo*, *Alvida*, *Montezuma* and others. (Don't worry if you've never heard of any them: you're not alone.)

Although you'd hardly know it nowadays, Vivaldi's popularity as an opera composer was unequalled by his contemporaries. Between 1713 and 1739, when he was actively writing for the stage, more of his operas were produced in Venice than those of any other composer. Even if we take a conservative number of operas – say 47 or 49, depending on who's counting – that still means he composed nearly two a year. He wrote his opera *Tito Manlio* in just five days, though that may not be anything to brag about. Towards the end, he began to take shortcuts. His last operas contain arias that were written by Handel, Pergolesi and other composers. Maybe Vivaldi had just had enough.[3]

Today the operas of Vivaldi are completely forgotten. As a composer, he's remembered entirely for his instrumental writing, especially such tuneful ditties as the collection now known as *The Four Seasons*. Cynics say he chose that title because he knew that the works would be played in the elevators of luxury hotels. This is clearly ridiculous: Vivaldi obviously chose the name because he knew the record jackets would have such pretty photographs.

[3] He's not the only one. Sir Neville Marriner, the famous conductor of the Academy of St. Martin-in-the-Fields orchestra, once said, "People can die from an overdose of Vivaldi. It makes you feel as though you are working in a sewing-machine factory."

A close shave with The Barber of Seville

ROSSINI

ROSSINI WAS THE PARTY ANIMAL of the Italian opera scene. He liked to flirt with pretty women, socialize with his friends and eat rich food. The best thing about being a famous opera composer, as far as he was concerned, was that he got to meet all the right people. Besides, it was easier for him to get a table at the best restaurants.

Gioacchino Rossini was born on the 29th of February, 1792, in Pesaro, a small town on the Adriatic coast. (It was typical of Rossini to be born in a leap year: he always was a practical joker. When he died in 1868 he was 76 years old and had celebrated only 19 birthdays.)[1]

The Rossini family had once been wealthy and important – an ancestor had been ambassador to the Duke of Ferrare and the family even had a crest showing a nightingale over a rose – but later fell on hard times. Rossini's father, Giuseppe Rossini, was the town trumpeter, the town crier and the official inspector of slaughterhouses. (You wanted to make sure your slaughterhouse was up to standard when Giuseppe Rossini came for inspection: if it wasn't the whole town might hear about it, complete with a trumpet flourish.) The composer's mother, Anna Guidarini, was a baker's daughter who became a dressmaker and

---

[1] He kept his sense of humor all his life. His last major work, written in 1864, is his *Petite Messe Solennelle*, a "Little Solemn Mass" that's neither little nor solemn (though it *is* a mass). The title page says it's written "for 12 singers of three sexes."

97

had a sweet singing voice. Rossini remained devoted to his parents his whole life. He wrote home regularly like a good boy.

Rossini studied music from an early age but didn't have much patience for book learning and theory. (His first piano teacher used to doze off in the middle of the lessons: when he woke up, the young Rossini would dutifully report that he had played all the pieces.)

He wrote his first opera when he was 14 years old, but that one hardly counts. It wasn't until after formal study in Bologna that his real operas started coming out.

Once he got going, there was hardly any stopping him: *La Cambile di matrimonio, L'Equivoco stravagante, Demetrio e Polibio, La Scala di seta, Il Signor Bruschino* – he dashed them off at a great rate, usually three or four in a good year. From 1810 to 1829 he wrote 40 operas. Then he quit.

Rossini wrote quickly and easily, and he didn't seem to care much what the subject matter was. "Give me a laundry list," he once said, "and I will set it to music." (Given some of the libretto texts he had to work with, he might have done better with a laundry list or two.)

He claimed to have written one overture – I wish I knew which one – in the time it took to boil a pot of rice. He composed the overture to *Le Comte Ory* in his head while fishing with his banker, Aguado, and dangling his feet over the side of the boat. Rossini liked to compose while lying in bed, and one story tells how he dropped a sheet of music onto the floor. Too lazy to stoop down to pick it up, he just wrote the whole aria over again. (I think he made this story up. It sounds too good to be true.)

One of the reasons Rossini could write so quickly, of course, is that he stole a lot of his music from himself. (Maybe a few times from other composers, too, but mostly from himself.)   His tragic opera *Tancredi*, first performed in Venice in 1813 and one of his earliest successes, uses the overture he'd written the year before for *La Pietra di paragone*. (Well why not? That had been in Milan, and the Venetians hadn't heard it yet.)

One of his biggest hits was *Il Barbiere di Siviglia* (The

Barber Of Seville), which he dashed off in just under two weeks in 1816 – prompting Donizetti to remark "I always knew Rossini was a lazy man." It has bits from all over, including the same overture he'd used the year before in *Elisabetta, regina d'Inghilterra* (and before that for *Aureliano in Palmira* in 1813 and before that for *L'Equivoco stravagante* in 1811. What can I say? He liked the tune.) When he wrote *La Siege de Corinthe* in 1826 he used the overture he'd written for *Maometta* in 1820.[2]

Most Rossini overtures follow a pretty predictable pattern: they start quietly and then get louder and louder until the big, splashy finish. This came to be known as the "Rossini crescendo" and earned him the nickname *Signor Vacarmini*, or "Mr. Noisy."

Rossini seemed to work best under pressure, even if that meant making his theatre managers into nervous wrecks. "Nothing primes inspiration more than necessity," he once wrote to a friend, "whether it be the presence of a copyist waiting for your work, or the prodding of an impresario tearing his hair.

"In my time," he bragged, "all the impresarios of Italy were bald at thirty."[3]

The impresario Domenico Barbaja got him back when it came to writing *La gaza ladra* (The Thieving Magpie) in 1817. Came the day of the opening night and Rossini still hadn't written the overture, so Barbaja locked him in an upstairs room with four hefty stagehands, who threw the pages of music as fast as he wrote them to a copyist waiting below. They had orders to toss out Rossini if he didn't finish it on time. (As far as I know he didn't even steal it from anywhere, which was awfully sporting of him.)[4]

Nowadays, we remember Rossini (if we remember him

---

[2] Several historians have accused Rossini of stealing the march section of this overture from Mayr. But Mayr had stolen it from Marcello anyway.

[3] In later life, Rossini himself went completely bald, and bought a whole bunch of fancy wigs.

[4] Don't forget about Barbaja: he shows up again with Bellini.

at all) mostly for his comic operas. But in his day he spent a lot of time writing serious stuff, including a religious opera on the life of Moses and a tragic opera based on Shakespeare, *Otello*, which was all the rage until Verdi's version came along some 70 years later.

The English poet Lord Byron, by the way, didn't care much for Rossini's *Otello*, which he says he saw "crucified into an opera" in Venice in 1818. When Byron died six years later in 1824, Rossini wrote an eight-part cantata for a memorial service in London, just to show there were no hard feelings.[5]

It was in Naples that Rossini met the celebrated soprano Isabella Colbran, who starred as Queen Elizabeth in his opera about the great English queen. Rossini had never been to England at that point, but that didn't stop him writing about it. (He'd never been to Algiers when he wrote *L'Italiana in Algeri*, either.) The story's a real potboiler that has nothing to do with the historical facts, but that's never bothered opera composers. Colbran was dark and haughty and Spanish and seven years older than Rossini, who found her quite attractive. Pretty soon they were having a fling, for which she dumped her affair with Barbaja. (He didn't seem to mind: the three of them stayed friends, and Barbaja even let Rossini share in a percentage of the profits from the gambling tables in the lobby.)

After living together for several years, Rossini and Colbran got married in 1822. He wrote many of his big, dramatic operas to show off her voice. (It was for *Elisabetta* that he got into the habit of writing out all the vocal ornaments he wanted, since he was tired of flashy singers trying to ruin his carefully composed melodic lines.) Another famous Rossini singer was the contralto Marietta Alboni, who eventually grew too fat to sing opera: she

---

[5] Byron – that rake, cad and womanizer – was a bit of a character. While a student at Cambridge, he kept a tame bear and a mistress whom he liked to disguise as a boy. He'd gone to Venice in 1816 after leaving England in a hurry because he'd been having an incestuous affair with his half-sister.

couldn't move and sing at the same time. She continued with a concert career, and did all her singing while seated in a big armchair. Rossini called her "the elephant who swallowed a nightingale."

In 1824, Rossini and his wife went to England, where they had a wonderful time rubbing elbows with the aristocracy. Rossini sang duets with King George IV and gave singing lessons to the Duke of Wellington. (The visit started badly: Rossini got very seasick crossing the Channel and spent the first week recuperating at an apartment on Regent Street with his pet parrot, looking out the window at the passers-by.) Rossini was in such demand as a party guest that he began to charge for his personal appearances. He made a small fortune that way.

Rossini was one of the most celebrated composers in all of Europe but even he had his brushes with failure. Take the production of his opera *Torvaldo e Dorliska* in Rome in 1815, which was such a disaster that after the opening night instead of his usual letter home to his mother he sent her simply a drawing of a badly blown wine bottle (the kind with the straw bottom that Chianti comes in). The Italian word for such a bottle, and such a mistake, is *fiasco* – and that's where we get the expression in English.

Probably the most famous Rossini fiasco was the opening night of *The Barber Of Seville* in Rome in 1816. Hardly anything went right: the tenor broke a guitar string, the bass fell through a trapdoor and had to sing with a bleeding nose, and near the end a cat wandered onto the stage, sending the audience into fits of laughter.

Actually, Rossini is hardly to blame. The whole thing had been a bit of a setup: jealous friends of the composer Giovanni Paisiello, who'd written an earlier version of the same story, came to the opening night to jeer and make rude noises. Their conspiracy did no good: by the second night, Rossini's Barber was on its way to becoming a great success, and nowadays hardly anyone has ever heard of Paisiello. (Rossini wasn't there for the more successful second night: he was at home pretending to be sick.) At the end of the run, a grateful Barbaja gave him a handsome nut-brown suit with big gold buttons.

Rossini wrote his last opera, *Guillaume Tell* (William Tell), in 1829.[6] He was 37 years old and he'd written 40 operas in 19 years and he'd had enough.

He retired, lived off his royalties and spent the next 39 years partying and travelling with friends, including a few of the Rothschilds (Rothschildren?).

Around about 1832, while visiting Paris, Rossini met Olympe Pelissier, with whom he began to spend an increasing amount of time. (Things weren't going so well with Isabella Colbron: she'd taken to gambling heavily.) Rossini and Colbron drew up a separation agreement in 1837 and he began living with Olympe Pelissier. They got married when Colbron died in 1854.[7]

Rossini spent his retirement enjoying himself. He became a gourmet cook and grew increasingly fat. On Saturday nights he'd host a music party to which anybody who was anybody would try to be invited. Sometimes Rossini would play piano, or sometimes Liszt or Saint-Saens would drop by.

Rossini was always a bit of a hypochondriac, but as the years wore on his health grew worse. If it wasn't one thing it was another. He'd picked up syphilis somewhere along the way.

Although he wrote no more operas, Rossini continued to compose, mostly small piano pieces to amuse his party guests. He called them "Sins of my old age." One set of piano ditties, called Hors d'oeuvres, included movements entitled Radishes, Anchovies, Gherkins and Butter. These, you might say, were his salad days.

---

[6] You know: it's the one about The Lone Ranger.

[7] Pelissier was a great support to Rossini. Once when Berlioz made a disparaging comment about one of Rossini's operas, she mailed him a package containing a pair of donkey's ears.

Keeping the home fires burning in Norma

BELLINI

MANY OPERA LOVERS CONSIDER Bellini the greatest composer of the 19th-century style of grand opera known as *bel canto*, which is Italian for "beautiful song." If that's what they think, who am I to say otherwise?[1]

Bellini didn't write nearly as many operas as his buddies Rossini and Donizetti, but then he did have a foolproof excuse: he died young. Bellini died in 1835 before reaching his 34th birthday, thus adding his name to the roster of famous composers who died before hitting 40: Bizet at 36, Chopin at 39, Mendelssohn at 38, Mozart at 35, Purcell at 36 and Schubert at 31, just to name a few. (Richard Strauss, by contrast, lived till he was 85, and Verdi died at the ripe old age of 88.)

At his death, Bellini had written only nine operas (by the same age, Donizetti had cranked out nearly 40 and Rossini nearly 35), but he tended to brood over them longer than the other guys. (Wagner, on the other hand, took 65 years to write only nine operas, for an average of about 7.2 years per opera. But then, his were longer. A *lot* longer.)

Anyway, no one could accuse Bellini of being the class clown. (He was a pretty serious fellow all around. Only one of his operas, *La Sonnambula*, could be considered comic, and even that one's not exactly a barrel of laughs.)

---

[1] Singers who aren't nearly good enough for this style could be said to belong to the *can belto* school.

Strictly speaking, Bellini wasn't an Italian composer, since he was born on the island of Sicily. But that's the sort of thing that usually worries Italians and Sicilians more than anybody else. I can never tell them apart.

Little Vincenzo Bellini was born in 1801 in the small village of Catania, where his father was a church organist. Bellini's father didn't want him to be a musician (he knew what it was like) but he finally relented and allowed the boy to go to Naples to study. (A generous Sicilian nobleman put up the cash, this being before the days of student loans from the government.) Bellini did very well at school. You know the kind: he sat at the front of the class and always knew all the answers. In fact, he was such a good student that his first opera, *Adelson e Salvini*, was produced in 1825 while he was still at the conservatory. Bellini got his first big break when Domenico Barbaja, the bigwig impresario who managed the opera houses of San Carlo in Naples and La Scala in Milan, commissioned the young composer to write for him. His opera *Bianca e Gernando* opened at San Carlo in 1826, followed by *Il Pirata* at La Scala in 1827. Bellini was on his way up.

About this time Bellini began an affair with Giuditta Turina, whose husband was a wealthy silk merchant.[2] This little fling lasted about five years. Bellini once said that he considered it "useful in protecting me from marriage." And this guy's supposed to be romantic.

Domenico Barbaja (1778-1841), by the way, makes an interesting study on his own. Barbaja (some people spell it Barbaia) started out washing bottles and waiting tables at a Milan cafe. But he made a small fortune when he came up with the idea of serving whipped cream on iced coffee or hot chocolate. Pretty soon all the fashionable cafes were serving his specialty.

Barbaja did some heavy-duty (and not always entirely legal) wheeling and dealing during the Napoleonic wars before taking over the gambling casinos at La Scala. From

[2] Her father was a silk merchant, too, which may or may not be significant.

casino gambling it was of course only a short hop to becoming an opera manager. As an influential impresario, he introduced major works by Rossini, Bellini, Donizetti and Carl Maria von Weber, among others. He also, you'll recall, introduced Rossini to his mistress, the Spanish soprano Isabella Colbran. She promptly married the composer and they lived together for the next 15 years. Small world.

Bellini's first really big hit came in 1831 with his opera *La Sonnambula*, or The Sleepwalker. The title role of the sleepwalking Amina was created by a flashy soprano with the singularly appropriate Italian name of Giuditta Pasta. She went on to create the title roles in Bellini's *Norma* and Donizetti's *Anna Bolena*. (Before her sleepwalking jaunt, Pasta had performed in an earlier Bellini opera about Romeo and Juliet. She played Romeo.)

Although Bellini's fame was already firmly on the rise, his biggest success was yet to come, in *Norma*, his weepily tragic opera about love, treachery and betrayal among the Druids of pre-Christian Britain. Correct me if I'm wrong, but I don't think anyone else has written an opera about Druids. The music for *Norma* was not entirely new: never one to let a good tune go to waste, Bellini stole the music for Norma's big Act I aria "Casta diva" from his earlier opera *Bianca e Gernando*. No one seems to have minded.

Always sickly, even as a child, Bellini fought a continual battle with tuberculosis that often left him tired and weak. He was the pale, ethereal type. His face had delicate features framed by a mass of light-brown, curly hair. Women thought he was adorable. (Heinrich Heine says "his features had something vague in them, a want of character, something milk-like." Bellini, he said, "looked like a sigh, in pumps and silk stockings." (Maybe he got silk at a discount through his mistress's husband.)

Toward the end of his life, Bellini grew unreasonably jealous of the success of Donizetti, whom he accused of plotting against him. But Donizetti was only trying to help. (When Bellini died in 1835, Donizetti wrote a *Requiem Mass* in Bellini's memory, just to show he was a good sport.)

Bellini composed two more operas after *Norma*, but neither of them could match its success. *I Puritani di Scozia*, written just a few months before his death from intestinal problems, includes a big "mad scene" for its heroine, Elvira, which was written eight months before Donizetti's famous "mad scene" for *Lucia di Lammermoor*. It's kind of unfair that the Lucia mad scene is more famous, considering Bellini did think of it first.

Although Bellini's output was relatively small, his operas are admired for their dramatic flair and especially for the beauty of their melodic lines. If nothing else, Bellini knew how to write a good tune.

All ears in Lucia di Lammermoor's mad scene

DONIZETTI

THE NORTHERN ITALIAN FARMING district of Ber-gamo is known for two things in the history of music: the 16th-century dance form known as the *berga-masca* and, a couple of hundred years later, the operas of Donizetti.

Domenico Gaetano Maria Donizetti was a local boy who made good. He was born in the town of Bergamo in 1797, went off to become rich and famous as a big-time opera composer, and then returned home to die in 1848. In the end, the composer who made his mark with the famous "mad scene" in *Lucia di Lammermoor* went a little bonkers himself and spent the last years of his life in an asylum. This is known as dramatic irony. Some might call it poetic justice.

Donizetti's family was not a wealthy one. His father, Andrea, worked in a pawnshop (a useful connection for a musician, in case you were ever hard up for cash and needed to put your instrument in hock) and his mother brought in a little extra money doing needlework until her eyes gave out. But despite their simple means, they did what they could to encourage the young Gaetano in his musical studies, beginning in Bergamo and later when the boy went off to Bologna.

Gaetano was one of six children, but the only other member of the Donizetti family who made such a big splash was Gaetano's older brother Giuseppe, who was also a musician. Giuseppe played flute in Napoleon's army band and eventually became director of music for the Sultan of

Turkey. He moved to Constantinople, where he wore a fancy silk uniform and got to call himself "Pasha."

After his Bologna studies Donizetti returned to Bergamo and began writing string quartets and some other music for the local amateur performing societies. But you can't make a living that way and Donizetti, who by now was nearly 20 and keen to make something of himself, knew he had better find a paying gig and fast.

He'd had no luck with his first attempt at writing opera, a juvenile work called *Il Pigmalione*. He based the story on the Pygmalion myth that was later made famous as a play by George Bernard Shaw, and even more famous as the Rodgers and Hammerstein Broadway musical My Fair Lady. (Shaw, by the way, dismissed Donizetti in his music criticism as little more than a capable but uninspiring hack. Shaw particularly objected to the "absurd flute tootling" of Lucia's mad scene.)

Donizetti's first big break came when he was commissioned to write an opera for Milan. Though only a moderate success, *Enrico di Borgogna* was the first Donizetti opera ever produced and it started the composer on a roll.

Between 1822 and 1830 he wrote 26 operas, from *Zoraide di Granata* to *Anna Bolena*. (He didn't intentionally compose them in reverse alphabetical order. It just looks that way.)

Probably none of them you've ever heard of, except maybe *Anna Bolena*, which started the Italian composer on a British history kick. He followed it up with operas about, among others, Queen Elizabeth I, Robert Devereux (one of Elizabeth's old boyfriends) Mary, Queen of Scots and, of course, *Lucia di Lammermoor*, based on a story by Sir Walter Scott. He even wrote one called *Emilia of Liverpool*.

Once he got started there was no stopping him. By the time he was 35 years old, Donizetti had written 40 operas, and it wasn't unusual for him to churn out three or four in a busy year. He wrote his comic opera *L'Elisir d'Amour*, his biggest hit of 1832, in about eight days. By comparison, the six weeks he took to compose *Lucia* seems like loving attention to detail. To save time, 19th-century historian Louis Engel tells us, Donizetti would often write all the dots on the musical staff first, and fill in the stems and flags after that.

All told, Donizetti wrote 70 operas, give or take a few, but only a handful of them have stayed in the repertoire. Stop me if you've hear of any of these: *Parisina, Tarquato Tasso, Il campanello di notte, Marino Faliero, Belisario, L'assedio di Calais, Pia de' Tolomei, Betley,* or *Gianni di Parigi.* No? Well, that's fame for you.

But you surely have heard of such Donizetti hits from his more mature years as *La fille du regiment, La favorite* (Donizetti wrote the entire last act in about four hours) and his comic masterpiece, *Don Pasquale.* Donizetti wrote four more after *Don Pasquale,* but they never caught on. The piano arrangement of *La favorite,* by the way, was done by Richard Wagner. He hadn't yet become famous as a composer and was hanging around Paris doing hack-work to pay the rent.

Donizetti's operas made him popular and rich, but his last years were a major comedown.

Usually a genial and level-headed fellow, Donizetti later took a turn for the worse. He'd always had a bad time with headaches (he suffered a particularly nasty attack when he was writing *Lucia* (which may explain the mad scene), but by the 1840s his behavior became quite erratic. (A bunch of friends once invited him on a picnic and asked him to bring the pastries. Stopping his carriage at the local bakeshop, Donizetti went in and returned with a box of goodies. Then he went and got another, and another, and another, wandering in and out in a daze buying pastries until his friends finally stopped him.)

He also suffered uncontrolable fits of rage and gave way to bouts of frantic sexual activity. "The excitement of his genital organs," says a doctor's report, "no longer allows M. Donizetti to resist the impulse of his desires." That's one way of putting it.

For his ailments the doctors prescribed enforced rest, foot baths, and lots of mustard plasters and leeches. They put leeches in his anal region and behind his ears to drain his blood, but it didn't do any good. (Leeches rarely do.)

Donizetti was moved to an asylum near Paris, but his

nephew Andrea got into an argument when he suggested moving him to more familiar surroundings in Bergamo. Donizetti's banker and his wife, August and Zelie de Coussy, thought he should stay with them in Paris. (Their motives weren't altogether honorable: August had gambling debts he wanted to pay off with Donizetti's money, while Zelie seems to have had something a little more physical in mind.)

But the nephew eventually won and Donizetti spent his few remaining months in Bergamo, where he died in 1848 and was buried in the town cemetery. Although it was probably a stroke that finally got him, the autopsy reveals that Donizetti's madness was a symptom of advanced syphilis, something he'd probably picked up without knowing it during his footloose student days. It just goes to show, you can never be too careful.

In 1875, 27 years after his death, Donizetti's body was exhumed so it could be reburied in a more elaborate memorial at the church of San Maria Maggiore. When they opened the coffin they discovered that the top of his skull was missing. It turns out it had been taken by Gerolamo Carchen, an Austrian military doctor who'd been watching the autopsy. He wanted it as a souvenir.

The skull cap spent the next 75 years on display in the Donizetti museum in Bergamo, before it was buried with the rest of his bones in 1951.[1]

In a solemn ceremony, the music scholar Guido Zavadoni attached the skull cap to the top of Donizetti's head with three pieces of adhesive tape. As far as I know, it's still holding.

I'm glad he's back together again and resting in peace, but I suppose you could argue that it wouldn't make that much difference. Being dead, Donizetti won't be writing any more operas off the top of his head anyway.

[1] The same sort of thing happened to Haydn, you may remember (or you would if you'd read my earlier book *Bach, Beethoven, And The Boys*). He died in 1809 but was buried without his head at all. It didn't catch up with the rest of him until 1954.

Silent scenery in Aida

VERDI

GIUSEPPE VERDI WAS BORN IN 1813, the same year as Richard Wagner. But we shouldn't hold that against him: after all, he couldn't help it.[1]

If anyone's to blame, I suppose it would have to be Verdi's parents (or maybe Wagner's). But even that doesn't seem very fair, considering what they were going through at the time.

Giuseppe Fortunino Francesco Verdi was born in the small Italian village of La Roncole, in the district of Parma, to Carlo Verdi, a grocer and innkeeper, and his wife, Luiga Uttini.

When Verdi was born, Parma was busy being invaded by the Austrians, who were trying to get rid of Napoleon's troops. (Continental Europe spent most of the early 19th century either being invaded by Napoleon, or being invaded by people trying to get rid of Napoleon. There was just no escaping him.)[2]

Verdi's birth certificate actually gives his name as Joseph Fortunin Francois, but 1813 in Parma wasn't the best of times or places to be carrying a French name, so his parents quickly changed it. (In English, Giuseppe Verdi's

---

[1] Verdi was born on Oct. 10, the feast day of St. Francis Borgia, who's the one you should pray to if you're worried about earthquakes.

[2] In my opinion, the majority of Napoleon's personality problems – his arrogance, his delusions of grandeur and his general pushiness – can be traced to the fact that he only slept about four hours each night. It made him cranky.

name would be just plain Joe Green.) [3]

The young boy got his first musical training pretty much the same way as the other great composers: it started early and led to a job as organist by the time he was 12. (Aspiring opera composers take note: this seems to be a sure-fire ticket to later fame and glory.)

Hoping to expand their boy's musical horizons, Verdi's parents packed him off to the nearby town of Busseto, where he lived at the house of another grocer named Antonio Barezzi, who ran the local musical society. Pretty soon the young Verdi was writing marches for the town band and all sorts of other music. But mostly what he wrote were piano duets for himself to play with Barezzi's attractive daughter, Margherita.

By 1832 – Verdi was now 19, if you've been counting – Barezzi decided there wasn't anything more he could teach Verdi about music and encouraged him to apply to the Milan conservatory. (Verdi obviously had a few more things to learn from Barezzi's daughter: they were married in 1835 and had two children by 1839.)

The conservatory teachers in Milan were duly impressed by Verdi's talents, but rules were rules: they told him he was four years too old to be accepted. (Verdi got back at them many years later, when he was a world-famous composer and he refused their request to name the conservatory after him. "They wouldn't have me young," he said. "They cannot have me old." So there.)

Discouraged but undaunted, Verdi went back home to Busseto and took private lessons. He composed his first opera, *Oberto, conte di Bonifacio*, for a performance in Milan in 1839. It was successful enough that the impresario Bartolomeo Merelli footed the bills and asked him to compose another opera, this one a comedy.

Bad move, as it turned out. It probably seemed like a good idea at the time, but shortly after he started writing it,

[3] Verdi and his mother escaped the Austrian troops by hiding out in a church belfry. He never went to church much after that.

Verdi's wife and children became ill and died. Verdi himself was feeling a little under the weather.

He got the opera finished, but needless to say *Il finto Stanislao*, later renamed *Un Giorno di regno*, was hardly a success. He just wasn't in the mood to be funny.

In fact, after the failure of *Un Giorno*, Verdi wrote no more comic operas until his very last one, *Falstaff*.[4] Verdi wrote *Falstaff*, based on Shakespeare's lovable rogue, when he was nearly 80 years old, and could afford to joke around a bit. (Falstaff ends with a fugue on the text *Tutto nel mondo e burla; l'hom e nato burlone:* "All the world's a joke; all men are born fools." That's for sure.)

All told, Verdi composed 26 operas, a whole bunch of which you've probably never heard of, like for instance *I Lombardi*, *Ernani*, *I Masnadieri* and an "occasional opera" called *La Battaglia di Legnano*. (If it was only occasionally an opera, I have no idea what it was the rest of the time.)

For his librettos, historian Donald Jay Grout tells us, Verdi stuck to "violent blood-and-thunder melodramas, full of improbable characters and ridiculous coincidences." Verdi believed in giving audiences what they wanted, not what was good for them.

The death of his wife and kids, coupled with the failure of *Un Giorno di regno*, made Verdi – understandably – something less than cheerful. He went away and sulked for nearly three years.

Merelli finally managed to get him back to work by tempting him with a brand-new libretto by Themistocles Solera, an up-and-coming Italian versifier. (Before becoming a poet, Solera had run away from boarding school in Vienna to join the circus.)

The new libretto was *Nabucco*, the story of a mad Babylonian king who converts to Judaism. Verdi composed a rousing chorus for the Levites in Act II and another crowd-pleaser, "Va, pensiero," in Act III and the opera became a big

---

[4]He wrote an opera about Joan of Arc and another one about Attila the Hun. Neither of them is funny in the least.

hit. Verdi was on his way to the big time.

After writing the libretto for Nabucco, Solera collaborated with Verdi on *I Lombardi, Attila,* and *Giovanna d'Arco.* He also composed an opera or two of his own, but nothing much came of them.

Solera later became a spy for Napoleon III and then the chief of the Egyptian police before settling in Paris as an antique dealer. (That was the great thing about the 19th century: there was so much more job mobility.) Solera died in Milan, penniless and forgotten. To the end, he was trying to find a buyer for a bust of Christ he was convinced was the work of the Italian master Benvenuto Cellini. It wasn't.[5]

Merelli was a pretty interesting character, too. He was born into a prominent family and his father wanted him to become a lawyer. But the small matter of a weekend visit to a count's estate and the question of some missing family silver put an end to that idea. Merelli decided that running an opera house was better suited to his talents anyway.

It was during the rehearsals for *Nabucco* in 1842 that Verdi became friendly with Giuseppina Strepponi, the soprano who created the role of Abigaille, the mad king's scheming daughter. But it wasn't until a few years later, when she had retired from the stage to teach in Paris, that they started living together. Eventually they even got married.[6] Verdi called her "Peppina."

By now, Verdi was dashing off operas at an alarming rate. Some of them were not very good, and he knew it. (One of them, *Alzira,* the composer himself described as "really terrible.") But they were good enough to increase his popularity and earn him enough money to buy a farm in the country near his old stomping grounds, Busetto. Every

[5] Hector Berlioz wrote an entire opera about Benvenuto Cellini, but it was a flop. He later threw a bunch of the tunes together and called it the Roman Carnival Overture.

[6] Some people will tell you that Strepponi had been having an affair with Merelli, and had the children to prove it. But that's just malicious gossip. The father of her two children was actually Napoleone Moriani, a big tenor and an even bigger cad.

time he finished another opera, Verdi would plant a tree to celebrate.

One of Verdi's most popular operas from this period is *Rigoletto*, the one about the hunchback jester, the lecherous Duke and the professional assassin with the cumbersome name of Sparafucile. One of Verdi's best-known tunes,"La donna e mobile," shows up in Act IV.

The libretto for *Rigoletto* is based on a Victor Hugo play that had scandalized audiences in Paris a few years earlier. At first, the official censor wouldn't allow Verdi to write the work, but he got around them merely by changing the names of the characters. Censors are not very bright: it's one of the job requirements.

Like all composers in 19th-century Italy, Verdi was constantly having run-ins with blockheaded censors over one thing or another. To keep the censors happy with his later opera *Un Ballo in maschera* (A Masked Ball), Verdi and the librettist Antonio Somma demoted the tenor hero, Riccardo, from an Italian king to a duke, then made him the King of Sweden. For the first performance in Rome in 1859, they made him an English count and set the whole story in Massachusetts. Somehow that made all the murder, adultery and witchcraft acceptable. Don't ask me how. Nowadays Riccardo's usually back in Sweden where he belongs.

Verdi had one of his best years in 1853, which saw him create two of his biggest hits, *Il Trovatore* and *La Traviata*.

He composed *Il Trovatore* in a mere 28 days, which is less time than it would take most people to figure out the plot. I've long since given up trying. It's the one with the Anvil Chorus in Act II and all the confusing gypsy curses.[7]

La Traviata, on the other hand, is at least easier to follow, if not any easier to believe. The libretto is based on an Alexandre Dumas novel about the courtesan Violetta (courtesan is just a polite term for prostitute) who falls in love with a young nobleman named Alfredo, who promises to make an honest woman of her.

In the end, she dies of a terminal case of tuberculosis,

---

[7] Having a gypsy curse at you is nothing to take lightly.

but not without singing an interminable farewell aria first.

Like Puccini's *La Boheme*, written some 40 years later, *La Traviata* is a quintessential example of everything that's ludicrous about opera. Here we have a woman, more than likely built like a small elephant, belting out big songs about how she's wasting away to nothing. Whoever coined the expression "The opera isn't over until the fat lady sings" probably had this one in mind.

The first performance of *La Traviata* in Venice in March, 1853, was a complete disaster. The tenor had a terrible cold and kept croaking all over the place. All in all, the audience thought Verdi's tragic opera was the funniest thing they'd heard in years. Salvini-Donatelli, the soprano playing the consumptive Violetta, was so hefty and healthy-looking that every time she sang, the audience burst into gales of laughter.[8] It was not a good sign.

But Verdi got the last laugh, and *La Traviata* has since become one of the all-time favorites in the operatic reper-toire and was performed to great applause all over the world (including a performance, Verdi writes in a letter, in the American city of "Nuova Jork.")

Verdi went on to write several more big operas before taking a few years off to retire to his farm and grow cab-bages. He also made wine, grew corn and hay and raised livestock. The accounts show that in a typical year he owned four oxen, 17 cows, 10 bullocks, 11 calves and six rams. (Apparently no sheep.)

He reluctantly agreed to serve in the newly formed Italian parliament and represented the Busseto riding for five years. (He always voted the party line, just to be safe. His only significant political act was to draft a bill suggest-ing free musical education in Italian schools. It was never passed.)

Now we come to the opera you've been just dying to hear about: *Aida*. What's there to say? It's the one with the elephants. (Maybe after *La Traviata* Verdi considered himself something of an expert on the subject.)

[8] Her first name was Fanny, which probably didn't help.

He started writing *Aida* in 1869 after the Khedive of Egypt asked him for an opera to celebrate the opening of the Suez Canal. The Khedive, being a khedive, wanted something really flashy and elaborate to impress the neighbors. Verdi was reluctant at first, but finally let himself be persuaded.[9]

The canal opened on schedule but the opera didn't: all the sets and costumes were stuck in Paris because of the Franco-Prussian War.[10] Anyway, the opera had its big premiere in Cairo in 1871 and the elephants behaved themselves and everything. The Khedive loved it. (Verdi didn't go to the premiere: he hated boats.)

Aida had its Italian premiere in Milan in 1872 with the famous soprano Teresa Stolz in the title role.[11] Almost everybody thought *Aida* was a wonderful opera, except for a few critics, who accused Verdi of becoming too much like Wagner. (Now, *that's* an insult!)[12]

Except for his *Requiem* in 1874, Verdi hardly wrote anything at all for the next 16 years or so. He took it easy, travelled around to attend performances of this opera or that one, and made sure his beard was trimmed for opening nights. (In his later years, Verdi looked a bit like Santa Claus.) And there was always the farm to keep him busy.

He came out of retirement to write operas of *Otello* in 1887 and *Falstaff* in 1893, which show that he still had what it takes. (He always wanted to write an opera version of Shakespeare's *King Lear*, but he never got around to it.)

Verdi died in 1901 in Milan, having written more successful operas than some of us will ever attend in our lifetimes. He remains one of the most popular and best-loved of all opera composers – especially by anybody who likes to see elephants on stage.

---

[9] Verdi wasn't sure what a khedive is, and I'm not either. But whoever this one was he was rich.

[10] I forget how that one turned out. Who won?

[11] Around about this time Stolz and Verdi had become, um, rather friendly.

[12] Arrigo Boito, the librettist of Verdi's last great operas, didn't think much of Wagner. He called him "Hybrid and monstrous, half-man and half-brute."

Warming up to La Bohème

PUCCINI

PUCCINI DIDN'T INVENT the idea of killing off the major characters at the end of the opera. Handel, Mozart, Wagner, Verdi and a whole slew of others had thought of it before him. (Sometimes they wanted to kill off the *performers*, too.) But what he lacked in originality, Puccini made up for in consistency. He perfected the idea of the dying diva to something of an art form.

In fact, it is the rare Puccini opera in which at least one of the major characters – usually a woman – isn't dead before the final curtain. Granted, both Minnie and the outlaw Dick Johnson survive *La fanciulla del West* (The Girl Of The Golden West) – though the same could hardly be said of most of the audience. And none of the characters in *Gianni Schicchi*, Puccini's only less-than-morbid opera, suffers anything much worse than a bad cold.

But the death toll in Puccini's other operas is pretty dependable. Even in *La Villi*, his very first opera, Anna dies of grief and her lover Robert dies of embarrassment.

Mimi coughs herself to death in *La Boheme* (something that should happen more often to coughers in the audience), while *Tosca* ends with its heroine leaping to her death off a handy parapet (which the stage designer has helpfully included just for the purpose). The heroine of *Madama Butterfly* despatches herself using the nearest sharp object (you might, too, if you had a son named Trouble), while Manon Lescaut ends her stint on stage by dying of exhaustion. (And by that time, many people who've sat through the whole opera know exactly how she feels.)

In fact, Puccini heroines are remarkably likely to kill themselves, making them a major insurance risk. The heroine's probability of croaking is especially high if she has given the opera its title. Liu, the slave girl in Puccini's final opera, *Turandot*, dutifully kills herself when it becomes apparent that Princess Turandot, the title character, is too selfish to do so. Despite this, there's never been, as far as I know, a pressing urge to re-title the opera.

Some Freudian should probably look into all this. Music historian Alfred Einstein hits the nail on the head when he writes of Puccini's "beguilingly tuneful operas with their overwrought orchestrations of sophisticatedly brutal texts." That's about the size of it.

All in all, of the 12 operas Puccini wrote, eight of them end with either the heroine or another major female character being knocked off – a death rate of 66 per cent. The central male characters fare quite a bit better, though even they depart at a rate of three in 12, or 25 per cent. And you can be sure that none of them dies of old age. It's murder, suicide or tragic illness all the way. Puccini was no dummy: he knew what opera audiences wanted to see. If he'd been born a hundred years later, he'd be making movies in Hollywood.

But Giacomo Puccini was born far from Hollywood, in the small Italian village of Lucca, where his family had lived for four generations before him. Puccini's great-great-grandaddy, whose name was also Giacomo, was the organist at the village church of S. Martino. He passed the job on to Puccini's great-grandfather Antonio, who passed it on to his grandfather Domenico, who passed it on to Puccini's father, Michele. (Domenico Puccini died mysteriously in 1815. People said he'd been poisoned. It must have been something he wrote.)

When *our* Puccini was born in 1858, the fifth of seven children, his parents named him Giacomo Antonio Domenico Michele Secondo Maria Puccini – making him a kind of walking family tree. (Puccini later had a son whom he named Antonio, thus starting the whole sequence over

128

again.)

With all of this musicality in his blood (his mother, Albina Magi, was also a musician), there was no doubt what little Giacomo was going to be when he grew up. Sure enough, by the time he was 14, Puccini had landed more than one organ gig in Lucca, including the family job at S. Martino, where presumably he had good references. (He also later had a job, one biographer tells us disdainfully, playing the piano "in a more unholy place," by which he probably means a brothel, or at least the neighborhood bar.)

Popular legend also has it that a boyhood Puccini once pawned some of the organ pipes from the church of San Paolino to pay for cigarettes. The missing pipes, we're told, forced him to create some odd improvisations on the morning hymn tunes. (Puccini never did kick the cigarette habit. A friend of the composer writes that "he smoked like a chimney." He bit his fingernails, too, though presumably not at the same time.)

But following in the family footsteps and becoming just another church organist was not enough for the ambitious Puccini. He was a rebel: he wanted to compose operas. Nowadays he'd have gone into music videos.

This was not entirely radical: some of the earlier Puccinis had written operas, though none of them had tried to make a career of it. But the young Puccini had studied the operas of his great countryman Giuseppe Verdi, saving up his lira and forgoing the odd cigarette for money to buy the scores in piano reductions. In 1876, when he was 18, he and a couple of the lads walked from Lucca to Pisa – a road trip of nearly 50 miles one way – to hear a performance of Verdi's *Aida*. (Puccini, we're told, "grew up under the shadow of Verdi." No wonder he sometimes felt he was in the dark.)

Hearing Verdi's masterpiece had a profound effect on the young man, who decided then and there that opera was where it was at. That fateful performance of *Aida*, Grove's dictionary tells us, "opened a musical window to him." All he needed now was something more like a door.

Maybe it was all those elephants, I'm not sure. But whatever it was, for Puccini there was no turning back. (It's significant to note, of course, that both young lovers in Verdi's opera – the Egyptian soldier Radames and the Ethiopian princess Aida – die at the end of the story. Puccini had obviously spotted a trend.)

Full of enthusiasm, the eager Puccini packed off to Milan, where he studied composition at the conservatory. He got financial support for his studies from his rich uncle, Nicolao Ceru. (Great-uncle, actually. He was a doctor who wrote a gossip column for the Lucca tabloid.)

Among Puccini's teachers in Milan was the composer Amilcare Ponchielli, the only composer of any consequence whatever whose first name is Amilcare. Ponchielli's best-known opera, *La Gioconda*, contains the famous "Dance of the Flowers." [1]

In Milan, the student Puccini lived the life of the starving artist, complete with garret, apartment, which he shared with his fellow student Pietro Mascagni. Mascagni later earned fame as a one-shot wonder for his opera *Cavalleria Rusticana*, an opera not about rusty cavalry, as you might expect.

No doubt these years were to prove useful to Puccini when he later came to write about starving artists in his opera *La Boheme*. Like the opera's character Colline, Puccini once pawned his coat for money. He wanted to take a ballerina for a night on the town.

At night, forbidden by their landlord to cook in their rooms, Puccini and Mascagni would take turns loudly playing the piano and singing to cover the sound of clattering pots and dishware. Puccini was a lazy student who spent a lot of time doodling in the margins of his school work. He liked to draw funny caricatures of his teachers.

Puccini wrote his first opera, a one-act ditty called *Le Villi*, while still a student. He entered it in a publisher's

---

[1] You know the one. It goes "Hello mudda, hello fadda/ Here I am at/ Camp Granada."

contest. It didn't win, but the opera impressed enough of the right people that he was able to have it performed and the publishing house of Ricordi commissioned him to write a full-length opera. Things were looking up.

This second opera, *Edgar*, seemed to have all the right elements (it ends with Edgar's lover Fidelia being stabbed by her jealous rival) but its debut at La Scala in 1884 was less than successful. Never one to mince words, Puccini himself later referred to this work as "*una cantonata*," or "a blunder."

Around about this time, Puccini met a woman named Elvira Bonturi Gemignani, with whom he became, um, rather friendly. Their baby boy Antonio was born in 1886.

Puccini's family, as you might imagine, was shocked. Great-uncle Nicolao even demanded his money back. I'm not sure whether it was because of little Tony, or Elvira's two previous children, or because she still had husband leftover somewhere. (He was a prosperous merchant but rather boring fellow named Narciso Gemignani and he doesn't have much else to do with this story.)

Elvira was Puccini's first great love – although, as it turns out, not his last. Elvira's husband finally died in 1904, after which time she married Puccini and tried to make an honest man of him. It didn't work.

Still in his death-and-destruction mode, Puccini composed *Manon Lescaut*, an opera that begins in France but ends on a windswept plain near New Orleans. No good reason, except that it gives Manon a better dying scene, which was a good enough reason for Puccini.

The opera was Puccini's first big hit, earning him 50 curtain calls on opening night. Spanish soprano Lucrezia Bori tells the story of meeting Puccini backstage at the dress rehearsal for her debut as Manon in a later performance, feeling especially proud of the beautiful dress she'd had made for the climactic scene. Puccini, a stickler for detail, told her the dress was far too lovely for a character who was supposed to be starving, penniless and wandering in the wilderness. So he threw his coffee at her to give it that "lived-in" look. Boy, was she mad!

131

Now Puccini was on a roll, churning out his three biggest operatic hits in a row: *La Boheme*, *Tosca* and *Madama Butterfly*. Each of them, true to form, ends with the death of its heroine. But it's not enough that they die. What's worse is that they take ages singing about it before they finally drop off.

The critics were less than enthusiastic about the first performance of *La Boheme* (they gave Puccini a hard time for those parallel fifths at the opening of Act III) but audiences have always loved it for its great drama and soppy romanticism. Personally, I have a hard time keeping a straight face through the ending of *La Boheme*. Call me a cretin, but the sight of a strapping 200-pound soprano belting out an aria about how she's wasting away to nothing just cracks me up.

While writing *La Boheme*, Puccini and Elvira had set up house at a little villa on Lake Massaciuccoli, so Puccini would be able to compose, free from the noisy distractions of the big city. But what he really wanted to do was go hunting and fishing. So he hired a boy from the nearby village to sneak into the music room in the morning and play through what Puccini had written so far. Hearing the music, Elvira thought Puccini was diligently working away, when really he was off shooting pheasant. He liked to gamble, too.

The opening night of *Madama Butterfly*, at La Scala in 1904, was a complete disaster, with members of the audience whistling and shouting and laughing through the whole performance. Jealous rivals had organized the fiasco to get back at the composer. He took the work back and re-wrote parts of it to improve it. He made it shorter, for one thing, which is an immediate improvement. The later version met with greater success, and with the royalties Puccini bought himself a yacht, which he named Cio-Cio-San, after Butterfly's Japanese name.[2]

---

[2] Even more than boats, Puccini loved cars. And motorcycles. Anything that went fast. He was also a gadget freak. In 1903 he injured his leg in a car accident and walked with a limp ever afterwards.

For wholesale bloodshed, it's hard to beat *Tosca*, the opera that music critic Joseph Kerman calls "that shabby little shocker." It ends with Tosca stabbing Scarpia, her lover Cavaradossi being shot by firing squad and Tosca jumping to her death. By the end, hardly anyone is left standing. Verdi had considered the story once, but even he couldn't stomach all the violence.

It was the Moravian soprano Maria Jeritza, by the way, who started the tradition of singing Tosca's big aria "Vissi d'arte" while sprawled on the floor. She hadn't intended to, but during the dress rehearsal the baritone singing Scarpia accidentally knocked her over, and Puccini decided he liked it better that way.[3]

Puccini was forever travelling around to attend rehearsals and performances of his operas. He loved to travel, and besides, it got him away from Elvira. (Elvira didn't come with him. She got seasick.)

Being away from home gave him a chance to fool around, which I'm afraid he did quite regularly. There was Lina Cavalieri, a singer in the New York cast of *Manon Lescaut*, and Sybil Seligman, who found the Italian composer far more dashing and interesting than her husband, a London banker. (In her spare time, Sybil liked to go lion-hunting.) Even after their affair ended, Puccini and Sybil remained close friends. He wrote her letters and signed them "Noti Boi."[4] And there were others I won't bother to mention. (Puccini once described himself as "a passionate hunter of wildfowl, opera librettos and attractive women.") Puccini travelled to Bayreuth in 1912 to hear *Parsifal*, but declined an invitation to meet Wagner's widow, Cosima Wagner, after the show. Puccini was embarrassed because the woman he was with wasn't his wife.

Puccini's womanizing, needless to say, did not please Elvira. But in at least one incident, her jealous suspicions proved groundless. She had accused him of having an

[3] Jazz singer Al Jolson's popular song Avalon is based on the Tosca aria "O dolci tacio."

[4] "Naughty Boy." Get it?

affair with Doria Manfredi, a young woman they'd hired as a maid.

Not content with badgering the woman into quitting, Elvira voiced loudly about the village her opinion that Doria was a tramp and a slut. (She wasn't very polite about Puccini either, but he was more used to it.)

Elvira's accusations so shamed Doria that the young woman killed herself. The Manfredi family took Elvira to court and sued her for defamation of character after an autopsy proved that Doria had died with her virginity intact.

The judge found Elvira guilty and sentenced her to five months in jail, with a fine of 700 lira plus court costs. But she didn't do any time. She and the family settled out of court. After that, relations between the composer and his wife were, well, strained.

This is just the sort of story, of course, that Puccini should have chosen for his next opera. It has everything: passion, jealousy, intrigue, suicide. It's a natural.

But the story presumably hit too close to home. So Puccini contented himself with writing *La fanciulla del West*, the only grand opera ever written about the California gold rush. It ends with the two lovers riding off into the sunset.

The premiere of *La fanciulla* in 1910 drew big crowds, because of course by this time Puccini had become the Grand Old Man of Italian opera. His hair had gone grey but he sometimes dyed it black to make himself look younger and he took to wearing a battered old felt hat everywhere he went. He even wore it indoors most of the time, but he probably took it off when he went to bed.

After that he wrote a small opera (small for Puccini, anyway) called *La rondine*, or The Swallow. Puccini must have been in a good mood, because nobody dies in this one, either. His next creation was actually three short one-act operas written as a kind of trilogy. *Il tabarro* and *Suor Angelica* contain the requisite murder and suicide routines, but *Gianni Schicci*, with its story of a scoundrel who tricks some greedy relatives out of their inheritance, is the closest Puccini ever came to writing a comic opera. It's worth a chuckle, maybe, but it's not exactly a real knee-slapper.

Puccini's final opera, *Turandot*, finds him back in form with a complicated plot involving intrigue, betrayal, jealousy and suicide. The usual stuff. It also features three minor characters named Ping, Pang and Pong. (Where earlier Puccini operas had been set in such far-flung locales as California and Japan, *Turandot* is set in Imperial China. Puccini liked to keep his audiences guessing.)

Puccini died in 1924 from complications of throat cancer. All those cigarettes finally got to him. *Turandot* was not quite finished when he died, and the opera was later completed by his younger contemporary, Franco Alfano.

Some say that Puccini was the last of the great opera composers, and that his death brought to an end the era of truly grand opera. Certainly nobody since him has managed to make quite so much noise about it all.

Puccini once wrote: "An artist seems to me to be a man who looks at beauty through a pair of glasses which, as he breathes, becomes clouded over and veils the beauty he sees. He takes out his handkerchief. He cleans his glasses. But at the first breath the absolute disappears."

There was nothing Puccini hated more than foggy glasses.

20th-Century Leftovers

Prokofiev juggles his Love of Three Oranges

EPILOGUE

Even many fanatical opera fans agree that, for all intents and purposes, opera died out at the end of the 19th century.[1]

After Puccini and Verdi and Wagner, there seems little point in going on. What most people wanted to do was to hear the same old operas over and over again. Considering some of the alternatives, who could blame them?

Some stubborn composers have refused to recognize this and written new operas anyway. Alban Berg's *Wozzeck* will turn your ears inside out, and he followed that one up with one that's even more of a *Lulu*. Serge Prokofiev's *The Love for Three Oranges* makes an interesting twist on the traditional "pants role" with the character of the Cook, a woman's role sung by a bass. (Well why not?)

Paul Hindemith ran into trouble with his opera *Neues vom Tage* for the heroine's aria praising electric heat over gas: "Constant hot water, no horrid smell," she sings, "No danger of explosion." At a performance in Breslau in 1930 the city gas company sued him for damages.

Surely the shortest opera in the repertoire, and therefore on principal one of my favorites, is *The Deliverance of Theseus*, written in 1928 by the French composer Darius Milhaud. It's about seven minutes long, which means that with the proper sort of intermission I can probably stay awake through the whole thing.

[1]And none too soon for some of us.

THE AUTHOR

DAVID BARBER would like to admit that he is a close relative of the famous American composer Samuel Barber, but honesty prevents him from doing so. Barber lives in Kingston, where he is an editor and writer on music and entertainment for The Whig-Standard. His two previous bestselling books – *A Musician's Dictionary* and *Bach, Beethoven, And The Boys: Music History As It Ought To Be Taught* – are also published by Sound And Vision. In his spare time, Barber is a freelance performer and composer whose works include two symphonies, chamber and choral works,numerous vocal-jazz arrangements – and no operas.

THE ILLUSTRATOR

DAVE DONALD can't remember when he didn't scrawl his little marks on most surfaces, so it doesn't come as much of a surprise that he now makes a living doing just that. He is currently balancing a steady job as art director for a Toronto magazine publisher with his other more abstruse artistic pursuits. This book represents Dave's third illustrative collaboration with David Barber.

Also by David W. Barber and Dave Donald

A MUSICIAN'S DICTIONARY (1983)

BACH, BEETHOVEN, AND THE BOYS:
*Music History As It Ought To Be Taught
(1986)*

by Dave Donald

HECTOR AND THE BIG HOUSE (1977)

WHEN THE FAT LADY SINGS
Opera History As It Ought To Be Taught

Published in Canada by

Sound And Vision
*359 Riverdale Avenue
Toronto, Canada, M4J 1A4*

First printing September, 1990
15 14 13 12 11 10 - printings - 9 8 7 6 5 4 3 2 1
95 94 93 92 91 90

Canadian Cataloguing in Publication Data
Barber, David W. (David William), 1958-
When the fat lady sings
Includes biographical references.
ISBN 0-920151-11-6

1. Opera - Humor.   I. Donald, David C.
II. Title.

ML1700.B37 1990   782.1'0207   C90-094983-X

Printed and bound in Canada by Metrolitho Inc.,